WOLF COUNTRY

by Ewan Clarkson

WOLF COUNTRY

A Wilderness Pilgrimage

Ewan Clarkson

DRAWINGS BY DAVID K. STONE

A Sunrise Book
E. P. DUTTON & CO., INC. · NEW YORK · 1975

Published simultaneously in Canada
by Clarke, Irwin & Company Limited, Toronto and Vancouver
ISBN:0-87690-170-4

Dutton-Sunrise Inc.,
a subsidiary of E. P. Dutton & Co., Inc.

Library of Congress Cataloging in Publication Data

Clarkson, Ewan.
  Wolf Country

  "A Sunrise book."
  1. Wolves.   2. Wildlife conservation—Minnesota—
Superior National Forest.   3. Superior National Forest,
Minnesota.   I. Title.
QL737.C22C57   599'.74442   74–28050

Although not usually at a loss for words, I find it difficult adequately to express my deep and heartfelt thanks to all those Americans who helped me on my pilgrimage.

I owe a special debt of gratitude to my editor and her delightful family for their welcome and hospitality, to Jeffrey and Odell Larson, of St. Cloud, for pointing out the way, to Dr. David L. Mech and his team on the Kawashiwi River, to Conservation Officer Ross, to Lloyd and Lorry Scherer, of Lutzen, and last but by no means least, to the Hansen family, Frank and Mary Alice, Karl, Nancy, Ranna and Bill, to whom this book is respectfully dedicated.

Ewan Clarkson
November 1974

Contents

WOLF COUNTRY

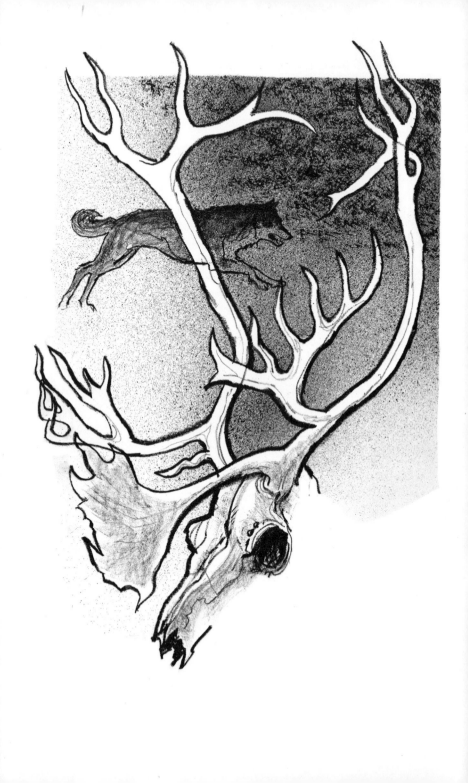

The Start of a Pilgrimage

The float plane banked and dropped, skimmed the spiky crowns of the tallest pines, and like a great gray goose alighting, came to rest on the calm waters of a narrow inlet. On all sides, the trees crowded down to the shore. In the sunlight and the silence, they seemed vested with an alien intelligence. They stood alert, watchful, seemingly resentful of this sudden intrusion into their privacy, and though a few leaned forward, as if curious to learn what manner of people had come to invade their wilderness, the rest, the greater majority of the waiting horde, stood aloof. There was no welcome from the trees.

In time, I was to grow to love the wilderness well, to become one with the silence, and to find myself imbued in some mysterious manner with the brooding calm of the North woods, but it was a long while before I could rid myself of the feeling that I was an intruder, unwanted, trespassing in an alien land.

For me, our arrival was an end and a beginning. It was the end of a journey, a long flight by jet plane, which had brought me across England and the Atlantic Ocean, over America to the plains of the Midwest, and then north to the forests of Michigan and Minnesota, eventually to lose myself in the vast sprawling wilderness that was the Superior National Forest. It was also the beginning of a quest.

It was, in a sense, a personal pilgrimage, a desire to see for myself, before it was too late, the grandeur of that wilderness which had shrunk so rapidly during my short lifetime. It was also a search, a journey undertaken in the hope of meeting the rightful heir to the estates of the North woods, a brother mammal, and a fellow traveler from the Pleistocene era, the American timber wolf.

Fate, it seems, has cast me in the role of the observer, and over the years, I have learned to put this trait to some use by describing, as faithfully and accurately as I am able, events and scenes witnessed from some remote mountainside, or recorded while huddled among the rocks in the teeth of a North Atlantic gale. Now, as I stood and watched the float plane depart, I realized that it was this passion for observing, this obsession, that had landed me where I was.

It was August, and I had turned my back on the glory of the ripening wheat and the high pageantry of summer in Britain. Soon the gray seals would be coming ashore off the rocky coasts of Pembrokeshire—the bulls to fight, and the females to bear their young. Soon the red stags would be belling and roaring in the combes of Somerset, and the swallows from the barn in my own Devon village would be gathering for their long journey south. Off the coast, the bass would be slipping like gray ghosts through the running green tide, and my boat was high and dry, swathed under a tarpaulin. My fishing rods were hung against the wall, and already my books would be gathering dust. It would be winter before I returned to Britain; meantime, I was thousands of miles from my native land, committed to a venture which at that moment appeared to be utter folly—a date, somewhere in the distant future, with a wolf.

Always, mankind has hated and feared the wolf. In the course of his evolution, man has overcome many other species, his peers down through the millennia. Some, such as the passenger pigeon and the great auk, he has exterminated entirely. Others, such as the buffalo and the blue whale, he has decimated to the point where they are perhaps no longer of ecological significance.

So far, man has failed in his attempts to exterminate the wolf. Failed, but only just. For no war waged by man against another species has been fought so long, or so mercilessly, as has his campaign against the wolf. Since before the dawn of history—when the pit, the snare, and the spear were man's only weapons—to the present day, when a light aircraft and a repeating rifle are not considered too expensive to be included in the range of weaponry, mankind has harried his arch enemy, the wolf.

All this carnage has been carried out without any hint of a moral code to temper the savagery with which man has pursued his end. No refinement of torture has been deemed too obscene, no way too devious to be worth exploring. Nowhere in the world has man ever learned to live with the wolf. Always the end sought has been extermination, and this end has justified the means.

Or has it? I was on my way to find out, and time was pressing, for already over the whole of the United States of America the wolf had been wiped out, annihilated except for a few bands scattered and hiding in the dense northern forests of Michigan and Minnesota. Does the wolf deserve his fate, or have we made a hideous mistake? Have we any right to decree the doom of the wolf? What, in fact, are the root causes of man's enmity toward the wolf?

Over and above these queries, there hung another question: What of the world of the wolf? What was the future of that vast immeasurable sprawl of lake and river, of swamp and muskeg, of trackless, impenetrable forest and old brown rock? Was that too, in peril?

I did not know, but again, I hoped to find out. I lived too, in the hope, presumptuous though it might be, that I could find some hitherto unnoticed pattern in that rich tapestry of interwoven life we are pleased to call the environment, some X factor in an ecological equation that would lead to its solution, and so help man to take yet another reasoned and logical step toward understanding.

The sun burned down out of a clear blue sky, but the wind from the north was cold with the breath of ice. I shivered, and I was aware of a deep feeling of regret that the wolf should have such an inadequate emissary. Suddenly I realized I was afraid, afraid of this alien land and the brooding mystery of its forests. I shook myself out of my reverie. There was a trail to follow and a camp to find before night. I shouldered my pack and set off.

2

Legacy of an Ice Age

We had come to an island set in a tideless sea. It lay sprawled in the waves, beached like some long dead saurian—its bones burned brown by the sun of ten thousand summers, its scaly hide nibbled and torn by the teeth of countless frosts. The island was Isle Royale, and the sea was Lake Superior, the largest body of fresh water in the world, its clear, cold waters spreading over an area of more than thirty thousand square miles and descending, in places, to a depth of more than thirteen hundred feet.

The lake and the island, and indeed the whole of the Northlands, were part of the Canadian Shield. The Shield is old, and it is mighty. It spreads over an area of almost two million square miles, and, in places, the rock dates back to the very dawn of time. Yet the story of the North woods, of its life and landscapes as they appear today, is very new, and it begins no more than fifteen thousand years ago.

It begins with the passing of the Ice Age, with the defeat—by sun and rain and warm, wet wind—of the great glaciers, the last legions of the Pleistocene frosts.

Before that the earth was cold, and it snowed. Far to the north, it snowed without ceasing, locking the moisture of the land into frozen crystals that built up, year after year, century after century, until by their own weight they compacted into ice, blue-white and cold, heavier and harder than rock. In that alien world, no life could survive. There was no sound save the howling of the wind, and nothing moved except the whirling, drifting, driving snow.

Then came a new sound, a sullen growl of menace and danger, as gradually, forced outward by the accumulation of its own weight, the ice began to move. It flowed southward, slowly, ponderously, yet with a force no power could resist. It tore deep into the earth, ripping away the yielding subsoil with icy claws and teeth, and pushing the debris before it as it crawled over the naked rocks. Even the rocks themselves were scarred, slashed and gouged as though savaged by some gigantic beast of prey. Ahead, like the wild outriders of some advancing army, bitter winds whipped away the dust-dry topsoil, spreading it far to the south to form the fertile plains of the Midwest.

In places, the ice was over a mile thick. Its weight forced the bedrock down. It bent the earth. Where the rocks proved too resistant to yield, the glaciers flowed on, forced uphill by the weight of the ice behind. At the summits of the hills, they were trapped but grew in size until they burst the rocky chains that held them and fell, taking with them the broken fetters of stone, only to shed them later on in their journey.

At last, the ice melted to form a vast sea, and as this drained away, it laid bare a landscape newborn, naked, and clean. In the hollows, lakes formed, their waters ice-cold, clear, and blue. Low hills, polished and rounded, stretched away to the horizon. Precipitous bluffs towered above carpets of fragmented rock, and huge boulders lay abandoned far from the rocks which had given them birth. Here and there, deposits of sand and gravel had been heaped into long ridges, or eskers, by the glaciers. Elsewhere, the rock was bare. Over all the sun shone, and the wind blew.

The wind brought the spores of life, and the sun nurtured them into growth. The spores were those of fungi and algae, neither of which could survive on their own, but which together formed lichens. They spread over the naked rocks, clothing them in robes of many colors—gray and green, orange and yellow, brown and brilliant red. The fungi reached down into the rocks, drawing minute amounts of mineral substances from the stone, while the algae tapped the energy of the sun to manufacture sugars. Between them, they began the slow, infinitely painstaking process of breaking down rock and creating soil, an inch every thousand years.

So the North woods grew, slowly at first, then in an ever-onrushing tide of life as plants and trees, birds and insects, reptiles and fish and mammals arrived, each to play its role in the ever-increasing complexity of the forest world. As life had begun, in unison and harmony rather than competition and strife, so each species came to join a cooperative community, each to occupy its own ecological niche, to draw from the common store of wealth the essentials of life, and, when death came, to repay its debt in full.

From the barren rock, a community had grown. It flourished, but it was fragile. The soil was thin and stony, lacking in humus and nutrients, quick to dry out after rain. The climate was harsh, and during the summer, the forests baked beneath a blazing sun, while in the winter the land lay locked in the grip of ice and snow, so that the processes of decay and regeneration, so vital to the build-up of the soil, were slowed down or stopped. Even the power of the sun was limited to a few short hours of daylight.

Yet for ten thousand years, the forests endured, while elsewhere in the world the earth trembled to the tramp of marching armies, nations rose and fell, empires were won and lost, and new religions were born. Already men had found their way to the North woods, journeying eastward across a narrow land bridge from Asia over a long-forgotten route now sunk beneath the waters of the Bering Straits. They came, but they were a gentle, selfless people, and, whether they realized it or not, they fulfilled the forest's one vital request. They took nothing from the North woods that they did not return.

Isle Royale, with its lakes and forests, its beaver ponds and marshes, was a microcosm of the North woods, and, in 1940, it became a national park. Much of its wilderness character remained intact. The Ojibway Indians had visited the island from prehistoric times to mine the copper there, but they had barely scratched the surface of the land in their search for the rich nuggets. Later, the white man, too, was attracted by the copper, but found mining there unprofitable. There was some pulpwood cutting, hunting, fishing, and trapping, but, in 1940, all this ceased. Now only fishermen reap a small harvest from the wild.

Wolves came to Isle Royale in the late 1940's, making the journey of some fifteen or twenty miles from southern Ontario across the frozen surface of the lake. Doubtless their ancestors had inhabited the island many times in the past, only to leave again, or be trapped, or shot. Records are scanty and vague, but it seems that prior to 1948, only occasional individuals had visited the island during the twentieth century.

Naturalists had several times advocated the artificial introduction of wolves to the island. As far back as 1934, A. Murie, who had carried out a survey of the moose population, had suggested that the herd would benefit from predator control in the form of a wolf pack. It was not until 1951, however, that the National Parks Service agreed to Isle Royale becoming a wolf sanctuary.

During the summer of 1952, the Parks Service attempted to

buy two pairs of wolf cubs, together with a wild trapped female, from Michigan bounty hunters. The cubbing season
passed without any success on the part of the hunters, and so,
on August 9, four zoo-bred specimens were obtained from the
Detroit Zoo and imported to Isle Royale.

Since the wolves were considered incapable of supporting
themselves in the wild, the plan was to rusticate them by
degrees, keeping them in pens and supplying them with food,
but allowing them to come and go as they pleased, in the hope
that they would gradually revert to the wild. Arrangements
were made with a Rock Harbor fisherman, one Pete Edisen, to
care for them in the early stages of their naturalization.

It soon became apparent that the wolves had plans of their
own. They began by harassing the Edisens, tearing up Pete's
fishing nets, and making off with several handmade rugs that
his wife, Laura, had laid out to air. They then turned their attentions to the camps of summer visitors.

The zoo-bred wolves were quite fearless, and accustomed
to being hand-fed. It can also be assumed that they were somewhat tactless in their method of approach, and since the timber
wolf may measure five feet from nose to tip of tail, stand thirty
inches high at the shoulder, and weigh seventy-five to eighty
pounds, it can be imagined that the presence of this quartet
around the picnic tables was less than welcome.

Pretty soon, the camps were in a state of siege. One elderly
professor, out for a stroll, was so persistently importuned that
he was forced to take to a tree, and to defend himself by
swinging his camera at the wolf. Unfortunately, he was so dis-
tracted he forgot to take a photograph! Nobody actually got
eaten, but many people felt that it was only a question of time.
In desperation, the Parks Service personnel trapped the wolves
and transported them thirty miles down the island. Next day,
they were back in camp.

Reluctantly, the National Parks Service decided to abandon

the experiment. One wolf they were able to trap and return to the mainland, but two had to be shot. The fourth escaped. This was an individual known as Big Jim. He had been hand-reared and was an excellent retriever. A year later, fishermen reported seeing a lone wolf swimming between two islands, but if this was Big Jim, it was positively his last appearance in public.

This abortive attempt to introduce wolves to Isle Royale was widely reported at the time, so it is not surprising that many people to this day believe that the island's present population of wolves is descended from captive stock. However, we now know that wild wolves were already present, and since all the captive females were accounted for, the wolves of Isle Royale may be considered truly feral, even allowing for the doubtful possibility that the blood of Big Jim lives on in some of the younger wolves.

In view of its history, Isle Royale seemed as suitable a place as any for me to start my explorations. I soon discovered, however, that although I might have come to the right place, I had come at the wrong time to see wolves. It was high summer, and every bush and plant and tree was in full leaf. The forest lay spread over the island like a thick, green quilt. Tall aspens and birches rose in slender columns to the skies, their trembling leaves a dense canopy through which the brilliant glare of the sunlight filtered faded, soft, and green. Spruce and fir and pine stood in dark, massy array, and where the light could penetrate, a dense ground cover of alder and poplar, beaked hazelnut and thimbleberry had sprung up. To step off the trail was to enter a dim, green, cavernous world whose walls were never still, where shadows flickered and moved and the light played a thousand tricks on the eyes. Here and there lay a bare outcrop of rock where crickets sang in the sun, or a meadow of sere yellow grass broke the line of trees, but over most of the island the forest reigned, two hundred square miles of dense, almost impenetrable growth.

Somewhere on the island, lost in this bewilderness of trees, lived the wolves of Isle Royale, perhaps twenty-one individuals all told. There were known to be a large pack of fifteen, a group of three, a pair, and a loner, but where they were at any given time one could only guess. They could travel for hours at a steady six miles per hour, and cover thirty miles in a day. They were also timid, and anxious to avoid contact with mankind. It was clear that I could spend years on the island, but unless I had an extraordinary run of good fortune, I would never catch sight of a wolf. In winter, when snow covered the ground and many of the trees were leafless, I might stand a chance of a fleeting glimpse, but the first snows would not fall for weeks, and the leaves had not even begun to flame with the fires of autumn.

Although it was after Labor Day and the bulk of the summer visitors had left, the island was still thronged with people. They crowded the trails, and in the evenings, the campsites rang with the sound of their voices, while above the clatter of cooking utensils and the thudding of axes, the blue smoke of their campfires drifted among the trees.

On that first evening, after I had eaten and rested, I retraced my footsteps a few yards back along the trail and struck off into the forest, making my way uphill. Slowly night fell, and a full moon rose white above the velvety darkness of the lake. I sat on a rocky bluff and listened to the soft sounds that whispered to me from the shadows of the trees, and I tried to lose myself in the spirit of the wilderness. I stayed for a long time, until the night wind grew cold and my aching limbs cried out for the warmth and comfort of my sleeping bag. The essence of the wild eluded me. Mankind was still too close. His presence filled the air and his thrusting vitality was alien to the fatalism of the forest. Each individual tried, in one way or another, to insulate himself from his environment, rather than abandon his identity and live as one with the earth and the sky and the silent trees. For me, at that moment, there seemed no place in either world.

3

The Secret of the Hills

I sat on a sun-warmed shelf of rock. Before me lay the sheltered waters of a narrow bay, where a flotilla of waterfowl, mallard, black duck, merganser, and a solitary loon lay at anchor, their silhouettes mirrored in the sunlit calm of the lake. Across the water, some half-mile distant, a series of low cliffs told of ancient shorelines, and days when the level of the lake was higher than it is today.

Beyond the cliffs, wooded hills lay spread beneath the faded blue of the sky. They shimmered in the heat, and it seemed to me that they beckoned and called as though trying to tell me they had something interesting to show me. Heat and inertia, coupled with the beauty of the lakeland scene, made me loath to move; yet, all the while, I felt a soft, insistent tugging, like the pull of a fish when it takes a bait in the darkness—invisible, intangible, yet urgent and demanding.

At last, I could resist the summons no longer and I set off toward the hills. The way led first through a swamp, where the tangled, twisted roots of alders lent precarious footholds above the ooze. I crossed an old abandoned beaver dam, its decaying logs held fast by a mat of turf. Brackish pools, their waters glinting in the sun, still lingered amid the reeds and grasses of the meadow, and the rotting trunks of long dead pines stood upright still, stark against the skyline. I climbed the crumbling wall of a cliff, and entered the forest.

Inside the woods, the air was as warm and stifling as a blanket. Dust motes danced in the rare shafts of sunlight that penetrated the gloom, and my feet sank into a soft, yielding carpet of moss. I pushed on, uphill, while infant pines pulled at my sleeves and snatched at the straps of my camera and binoculars. Only the thin scraping call of a jay broke the silence.

A woodpecker fled through the trees, his piebald plumage and startling red cap vividly at odds with the green of the pines. Then he vanished as he pitched on the trunk of a paper birch, and his markings blended with the bark of the tree. Even his red cap might have been overlooked or mistaken for some scarlet fungoid growth.

Now I was lost deep in the hollows of the hills, but I wandered on, with no clear objective in mind, picking my way through the trees, now clambering over a deadfall, now bent double to thrust my way through a tangle of low branches, now detouring to avoid a patch of soft ground. In one respect, I was grateful, for this was a very kindly wilderness. There were no thorns to puncture my flesh, no stinging plants, no briers to tear my skin. There were no insects either. At least I had chosen the right time of the year in that respect, for if I had arrived in early summer, I would have had to endure the misery of the bug season.

I came upon a patch of blueberries, fat and ripe, their soft, rounded skins warm from the sun. I burst them against the roof of my mouth with my tongue and savored the sweet juice mingling with my saliva. Suddenly, I was in step with the wild, my whole being attuned to the rhythm of the forest. I had lost all sense of time, all motivation. Now that I had no schedule to keep, no mission to fulfill, the forest ceased to hamper and restrict me, and allowed me instead to wander free.

It was then that I came upon the kill, or rather what remained of it—parts of a skeleton, some matted hair, and a hoof, all that was left of a moose calf that had fallen prey to the wolves. It lay in a clearing, among the moss and fern, and a small wreath of bunchberries shone scarlet amid the white of the bones.

I sat down on a log and picked up the hoof. It was small and cold and lifeless, and fitted into the hollow of my hand. As I held it, I realized that then and there, whether I was ready for it or not, I had to face the fact that the wolf is a killer. I sat for a long time, trying to recapture the last few moments in a life that can scarcely be said to have begun.

It happened here, in this clearing, in the cold light of early morning. The moose calf is crouched among the dead fern. Close by is the comforting bulk of the cow, and the air is strong with the smell of moose and the sweet, cloying scent of milk. There is a crashing in the bushes and a great lurch of fear as the clearing is filled with fleeting gray shapes. The cow bellows and wheels to attack, buffeting the calf as it rushes to her side. Then a battering and a banging and fiery spurts of pain as the calf is pulled away from its mother. A great weight bears it down into a roaring darkness and a suffocating red sea. Then pain and shock and fear are past and the moose calf is no more.

It all seemed quite pointless. Even if I ignored the evidence of pain—of the physical torture inflicted on a defenseless calf—even if I forgot about the sense of loss endured by the mother, the killing of the calf remained an act of vandalism, a criminal waste of the time and effort spent in the construction of such a complex and exquisite organism. I thought of the growth of the calf in the womb, of the long, slow passage of winter as the mother grew heavier with the weight of her offspring, the hours spent in the painstaking search for food, for such browse as remained available amid the snow and ice. Finally, with the coming of spring, there was the effort of labor and the birth of the calf, the awakening of maternal love in all its protective wonder. All this, torn apart in a few moments of ravenous greed.

Concepts of bounteous nature and of the prodigality of her spending rang singularly hollow and false, especially here in this North woods environment, where all the evidence pointed toward frugality and a meticulous balancing of the books in an economy which could only avoid bankruptcy by permitting no waste. In any accounting system, the loss of the moose calf had somewhere to be balanced by a credit gain.

Seated on my log, I pored over the evidence, studying the ledger of the wild, like some shirt-sleeve accountant who works alone on into the night, bent over his books long after the rest of the office staff has gone home. Suddenly, I saw my error. It leaped out at me, just as a wrong entry hiding in a column of figures suddenly reveals itself to the patient examiner. I had made my entry in the wrong column. The death of the moose calf was a credit in the environmental accounts. Its short life was the debit.

Hitherto, by some process of anthropomorphism, by a false sense of proprietorship, I had thought of the environment as existing to support the species, the forest to support the moose, the prairie to support the buffalo, the lake to support the trout. Anyone who owns a field values the land in terms of the amount of livestock it will support. If he is concerned about the fertility of the land, it is only in order that it might support more stock, which, in turn, will increase his wealth. Until now, my concept of the role of the wilderness had been no more than a wider application of this thought.

What if the reverse were true? What if the moose existed solely to serve the forest, was permitted to survive only for as long and so far as it could best serve the rest of the living world? Then the death of the calf made sense, and the wolves became key factors in a plan as brilliant as it was complex.

The assets of the environmental economy lie in its raw materials—in the metals and the minerals and the salts, the copper and iron, the potassium, sodium, calcium, and boron—all the building materials with which plant and animal can harness the energy of the sun and enrich the earth. In life, these raw materials are loaned out and locked in a deposit account in the structure of the individual, in the bones of the moose and the bark of the willow tree, in the feathers of the woodpecker and the fur of the beaver. In death they are recalled, recycled, to live anew.

The moose calf was conceived in the fall, as the maples flamed and the first fingers of frost began to edge out over the waters of the beaver ponds. In the warmth and security of the womb, the embryo grew, while in the world outside, the snow fell, the leaves withered and died, and the richness of summer dwindled away as all growth ceased.

Throughout the winter, the mother browsed on soft shoots of willow and aspen and hazelnut. She ate the needles of balsam fir and cropped the fronds of American yew. The bulk of her diet consisted of cellulose, of no direct value to her as food, but the moose was a ruminant, and her stomach contained bacteria which broke down the cellulose and converted it into food for themselves. The bacteria were, in turn, digested by protozoa, which were then assimilated as nourishment by the moose. Some of this nourishment reached the calf, and as the winter passed, the developing embryo grew deeper in debt to the environment.

The debt collectors came in the spring, a few weeks after the birth, and the calf paid in full. By a long and complicated process of biochemical interaction, the environment had collected a rich reserve of its mineral assets, assets which had lain scattered around, locked in twig and bark and bud. These assets had been carefully processed and prepackaged, and delivered just when they were most needed for instant use. The moose calf, the product of a winter's feeding among the snows, was now ready for its final processing before its return to the environment, and its distribution, to spread richness and wealth throughout the young, thrusting growth of the short summer.

The wolves played their part, reducing, by the aid of their digestive systems, the moose calf to the potash and phosphates and nitrates, and all the other mineral salts and trace elements from which it was made, and nothing, not a single atom, would go to waste. The sacrifice, although infinitely small in relationship to the great weight of the pyramid of life, was significant.

It seemed impertinent, even blasphemous, to inquire into the ultimate purpose of this intricate pattern of life and death. I could only see that it was so. It was the law, immutable and unchanging, and all life was subservient to its rule.

The afternoon was passing, and the shadows lengthened among the trees. I stood up and went to throw the hoof back into the ferns. Then I changed my mind and put it in my pocket. Back at the camp, I stood again on the rock and looked out over the bay, back to the forest hills. The sun had set, and the land lay dark and brooding. The hills had told me their secret.

4

The Festival of Youth

Moonlight filtered through the trees. The trail shone silver and the trunks of the aspens glowed softly white. Pools of shadow spilled out from beneath the rocks and the caverns of the forest were dark and impenetrable. All around, the night whispered and sighed with small sounds—a rustle and a scurrying, a trembling of dry leaves.

A deep, coughing grunt echoed through the darkness. The sound, repeated, drew nearer, traveling at some speed. A shadow denser than the rest emerged from the edge of the trees; and suddenly, a bull moose stood dark in the moonlight, his vast bulk blocking the trail. It was a moment for prudence and caution, for the bull was aflame with the fires of the rut, without fear, and prone to attack on sight. For perhaps half a minute, he stood in silence, alert and listening, before fading once more into the darkness of the forest. I heard the rattle of his antlers against the branches and the deep belling note of his call, then that too died away and he was lost in the silence of the trees.

It is difficult to believe in a moose, even when you see

one. It is as if all the leftovers of creation have been combined
to make this creature with its long, stiltlike legs, the body of
an ox, the neck of a horse, the head of a camel, and the ears of
a mule. Crown that lot with massive twin rosettes of spreading, palmate antlers, and the result is a herbivore weighing up
to half a ton, so successfully adapted to forest life that he
circles the globe—from Norway, eastwards through Russia
and China to Alaska, across Canada, and into the northern
United States.

Moose came to Isle Royale at the turn of the century. At
that time, great changes were taking place in the forests of
Minnesota and Ontario. Millions of acres of virgin timber were
being felled to meet the lumber demands of expanding civilizations, and moose were finding rich feeding in the lush secondary growth that sprang up following the activities of the
loggers.

As the numbers of moose along the northern shore of Lake
Superior increased, some must have swum out to Isle Royale.
Here again, they found plenty of browse and freedom from
predators, so for a time, the population prospered, until by the
1930's, most of the available food had been eaten, and the
moose began to starve.

In 1930, there may have been five thousand moose on the
island. Estimates are vague, but certainly by the spring of
1934, most of the browse was gone, and emaciated corpses lit-
tered the forest. By 1936, the number of moose surviving was
down to less than five hundred; but twelve years later, the herd
had again grown to around eight hundred, and another wave of
death reduced their ranks. Then the wolves arrived, and under
their control, the moose population grew more stable, although, after a quarter of a century of predation, there are
signs of a slow but steady rise in numbers.

The moose are not easy prey, nor is it likely that they fear
the wolf. Rather, all the evidence tends to suggest that the re-

verse is true—that a young, healthy moose has nothing to fear from the wolves, that he knows this, and has come to regard the wolf population as a nuisance, rather than a threat to his existence. Moreover, he asserts this confidence in a manner which causes the wolf to treat him with a profound respect.

Each summer, about two hundred and thirty calves are born on Isle Royale, and of these, about a hundred and forty are killed before the end of their first year of life. If the calf can survive the first few weeks of life, the odds in his favor soon begin to lengthen. Although he is not yet strong enough to defend himself against attack, the young moose is swift and agile, and as long as the lakes and beaver dams remain free of ice, a moose can always evade pursuers by taking to water.

Throughout his first winter, the moose remains in the protective company of his mother, and when he is a year old, a fresh crop of calves arrives to divert the attentions of the wolves. At the end of his second winter, though not yet fully grown, the young moose is rough enough and tough enough to take care of himself. It is quite possible that a moose fleeing from a wolf pack is motivated, not by panic, but by confidence in his strength and vigor, and his emotion during the flight is not fear, but rather an exhilaration of spirit inspired by his speed.

If, as often happens, the moose chooses to stand at bay—to defy his attackers rather than flee them—he must do so either because he is a very stupid moose, or else because he is assured that he is more than a match for the wolves. Stupid moose, like any other stupid animal, do not last very long, so the self-assurance of the moose must be well justified. The wolves know this, and acknowledge this superiority by stepping aside.

The years pass by, and the confidence of the moose in himself remains undiminished. Yet all the while he is increasing his debt to the environment, and the environment is mindful of what he owes. There is little room in the economy for either the very old or the very large. A few exceptions are tolerated, but, on the whole, the environment prefers to invest in the small and the swift, in the rapid turnover of life and death, and the mounting dividends of vigorous, soft young growth, rather than any long-term securities, however gilt-edged they may be. So, long before mankind formed the concept, the environment adopted the policy of built-in obsolescence.

Left to itself, the moose might well live fifteen or twenty years. As it browses, however, it inadvertently ingests the fertile eggs of a tapeworm, the *echinoccus granulosa*. These eggs hatch into tiny larvae, which migrate to the lungs and liver of their host. Here they form cysts, which grow as the larvae proliferate inside, and slowly the organs which support these parasites begin to degenerate. The moose is perhaps not aware of what is happening to it, but, gradually, its strength and vitality are being sapped.

The moose may not realize that he is gradually growing weaker, but the wolves know. They have probably encountered this moose many times in the past—in the course of their ceaseless patrols around the island—and their powers of observation are so acute, their sense of judgment so finely attuned that they are quick to detect the slightest signs of degeneration.

The wolves do not appear deliberately to seek out prey, but any potential victim they encounter is tested for speed and strength. Unwittingly, the moose betrays itself, perhaps by an air of indecision as to whether to stand at bay or run, perhaps by an initial lack of speed or by its stumbling, faltering gait. The wolves see the signs and press home the attack.

The end, when it comes for the moose, is not necessarily swift or painless. The wolf cannot kill quickly; he can only worry and tear, biting and slashing at the face, muzzle, and flanks of his victim until it dies. Death is due to shock, exhaustion, and loss of blood, accelerated perhaps by the strain on a heart already overtaxed by the presence of those same parasites that have rendered the moose liable to attack.

The wolf is a killer, yet innocent of murder. He cannot be condemned. As he stands in the snow, his tail wagging as he waits for the moose to die, he regards his victim with the same air of pleasurable anticipation as diners in a restaurant await the arrival of their steaks.

It would be easy to suggest that herbivores such as the moose do not feel pain to the extent that we humans do, but while there is some evidence to support the theory, it remains too easy an assumption, too facile, to be readily accepted. Furthermore, it is a dangerous assumption, for if it were generally accepted, it could be used to excuse widespread brutality and petty cruelty on the grounds of "They don't feel anything anyway."

The idea that the wolf is, in reality, a benign butcher may only be entertained when one considers the alternative. Left to itself, the moose would die a slow death, not measured in hours or minutes, but long days and weeks of misery. Weak, emaciated, his whole being permeated by the presence of parasites, each indrawn breath a rasping, wheezing gasp, left to cling to the last hideous vestiges of life, the moose would become a pitiable object indeed. Better by far that he should die in rage and anger, and, perhaps, who knows, right at the end, astonished disbelief!

The moose I met in the moonlight, in my eyes so majestic, so awe-inspiring in his might, could well prove, under the discerning gaze of the wolf, to be past his prime. At the end of seven years, the moose is obsolete, and yet, but for the intervention of the tapeworm, he might live three times as long. It seems important to the environment that three generations of moose should walk the earth, where one alone could occupy the same amount of space and time. Over and above the demands of the environment for the recycling of energy lie the

laws of evolution, and three generations allow for a greater
number of permutations in the lottery of genetics than one.
The first law of evolution is that the individual is subservient
to the species. The second law is that the species is subservient
to the rest of the living world.

The moose is dead and the wolf pack dines, bolting down
the hot flesh in great unmasticated lumps, hide, sinew, flesh,
and viscera—including the worm-infested lungs and liver.

Now the wolf becomes host to the tapeworm, for it is in
the intestines of the wolf that the parasite assumes its adult, or
reproductive form; in due course, the wolf will shed the fertile
ova in its droppings. In the interval, the wolf may have traveled many miles, thus insuring an even distribution of the eggs
which, in time, will be ingested by another moose. Thus,
unwittingly, does the predator sow the seeds of destruction for
its prey.

The ecological role of the tapeworm is clear, yet around
this role is wrapped another, greater mystery. The tapeworm
expedites the death of its host, and so hastens its own destruction. Yet it would be nonsense to suggest that it chooses so to
do, or that it is cognizant of its fate. The question remains:
What guides the tapeworm through the body of its host to the
site which best serves the interests, not of itself or of its host,
but of the environment?

Any answer, in terms of physiology or biochemistry, any
explanation by way of chemical attraction or repulsion,
seemed to me to be little more than scientific quibbling, solv-
ing one riddle only to be confronted with another, deeper conundrum. Slowly I was being forced to a conclusion, one that
I was at first curiously unwilling to accept. Somewhere behind
the moose, the wolf, and the tapeworm lay a guiding force at
once omnipresent, omniscient, and omnipotent, the physical
manifestation of which was the living environment, a power

for which no venture was too vast or too complex, nor any detail too minute to be of significance.

Slowly we are coming to look at the theory of evolution with fresh insight and to rewrite the story of survival. Where once we saw strife, we now see harmony. What was once believed to be dominance, we now know to be subservience. Where once we recognized that the parasite is dependent on its host, we now perceive that the host is also dependent on the parasite.

As the individual serves the species, and the species the environment, so too, perhaps, the environment exists to serve. If so, then all the evidence points to the fact that the environment is in the service of youth, that strength, in the wild, is not measured in terms of close-grained, knotted oak and resistant rock, but rather in the unfolding fronds of fern, in the bustling vitality of the nesting bird and the foraging squirrel. The strength of the environment is the strength of life, and life is most forceful, most vigorous, in youth.

Beyond that, I could not see, but it seemed to me that an eternal festival of birth and growth, of health and joy manifested in perpetual pulsing life, was no bad way for the world to turn.

5

Of Wolves and Moose

No rain had fallen for some time. The island was hot and dry, the trails bare and dusty from the passage of booted feet. Only here and there, in the depths of the forest that the sun could not reach and where the wind could not blow was the ground soft enough to bear the imprint of tracks.

Moose trails were everywhere. Each dawn, dark runways through the dew-drenched vegetation marked the passage of the great beasts during the night, and the slots of their cloven hoofs were sunk deep in the soft, spongy margins of the swamps. I searched for a long time, however, before at last I found, in the soft, bare mud surrounding a small spring, the unmistakable print of a wolf.

It was quite fresh, and I felt for a moment the taut tingling of nerves, the awareness of the hunter as he draws closer to his prey. For a long time, I stared about me in the faint hope that the owner of the print might be near, watching me from some rocky bluff or looking out from among the somber pines. Then I looked again at the print, and my hopes faded, for as I studied it, I realized that it was several hours old. Tiny, dried flower petals overlaid the smooth impression in the mud. It must have been made during the night or early in the dawn, and the sun was now high.

Not for the first time, I cursed the crowded confines of the forest and the dense tangle of vegetation that shrouded this land with secrecy. I found myself longing for a high mountain, the broad sweep of a hill, and a rocky, barren amphitheatre that I could overlook, where I could wait with my binoculars, watching from dawn to dusk as I had done so many times before. I found it hard to accept that it was easier to watch wild animals in ancient, overcrowded England than it was here in the North woods. Always before, it had been simply a matter of patience and perseverance. Now, it seemed, I had to rely almost entirely on luck.

The wolf that had left this print might now be many miles away. Even if he lay close by, he was as invisible to me as if he inhabited another planet. For every square mile of forest, there were at least two moose; yet, for all their numbers and their vast bulk, they managed effectively to conceal themselves. In three days, I had seen only one. Each wolf, smaller and infinitely less conspicuous, had ten square miles in which to hide.

A mere twenty-one wolves seemed totally inadequate to control such a large herd of moose, yet the mathematics made sense. The wolves probably knew every moose on the island, had tried and tested each one, perhaps three times in the year. To find a suitable victim, they might have to check more than a dozen moose before they came across one that betrayed its failing health. Even in the summer, in the days of the calf bonanza, the wolves might well take only those calves whose mothers were not at the peak of physical condition.

Over the year, the wolves might account for about a hundred and forty calves of all ages up to one year and at least eighty adults, yearlings or older, the majority of which would have some debilitating condition that would render them vulnerable to attack. Certainly, under such close scrutiny and pressure, no unhealthy moose would go undetected for long.

The slaughtered moose, large and small, provided the wolves with about ninety thousand pounds of meat in a year. Each wolf therefore consumed about four thousand five hundred pounds of meat yearly—nearly thirteen pounds each day. Even so, in spite of this predation, there were signs that the moose herd was growing at the rate of a few individuls each year.

It was pretty clear that the dynamics of the wolf/moose relationship were in a delicate state of balance. One extra wolf in a pack would ensure that the moose herd would remain stable, while two wolves would, in theory, cause a gradual decline in the numbers of moose. Yet no such decline was taking place. The wolf packs have been on Isle Royale for a quarter of a century, but their numbers do not appear to have increased. They must have bred, for the wolf does not survive more than ten or a dozen years, and the wolves now hunting the moose had to be offspring from the original pack. Yet the population remained stable.

From time to time, a wolf must get killed by a moose, especially in his early years, when he is young and inexperienced. Yet on each of three successive winters, the number of wolves counted remained exactly the same. Could the exact number of casualties be replaced by cubs? It seemed highly unlikely, but strange things happen in the wild.

In considering the delicacy of the balance between wolf and moose, there was a third factor to be assessed. The forest was maturing. In the early thirties, the woods had been cropped bare by a population explosion amongst the moose. Then a fire had swept over a large part of the island, and new growth had sprung out of the ashes to provide readily available browse for the few surviving moose. Three decades had passed since that time, and the new trees had grown up tall, their foliage out of reach. Now that the island was a national park, it was unlikely that fire would rage unchecked again, and so, with each succeeding year, the moose herd would have to work a little harder to find nourishment.

In summer, when every leaf and twig and bush is rich and green, when the lakes and beaver dams are choked with lilies and water weeds, when the berries are ripe and the squirrels fight over the pine cones and hazelnuts, it is hard to envisage a moose starving or a wilderness barren of food. It is in late winter or early spring, when the days are short and the water is locked in iron bands of ice, when the bare twigs of the willow or the dark needles of the balsam fir are the sole source of nourishment, that the wealth of the wild must be assayed. February, March, and April, these are the months of endurance, of hollow flanks and empty bellies, and perhaps, just as the warm breath of spring stirs the tops of the pines, a frozen corpse in the snow.

A fully grown moose needs at least twenty-five pounds of food a day. In summer, when the browse is full of moisture and much of his diet consists of aquatic weeds, the moose may eat thirty or forty pounds of greenstuffs in twenty-four hours. To support its moose herd then, Isle Royale must produce, in its short growing period, nearly six million pounds of browse a year, fifteen tons per square mile, or fifty pounds an acre.

No one yet knows how much browse the forest yields. Fifty pounds from an acre seems ridiculously small in August but, in March, it might take some finding, and any signs of overbrowsing in summer must surely portend hard times for the animals in winter. For the cow moose, such a winter could be doubly hard, for in addition to supporting herself, she needs to find nourishment for the calf growing within her.

Here again, the dynamics of the wolf/moose relationship, though perhaps oversimplified, are clear. If the moose population outgrows the available vegetation, many moose are going to be emaciated and weak and fall easy victims to the wolves. The wolves, in order to maintain their average yearly consumption of meat, are going to take a greater number of individuals than usual and so restore the herd to more healthy proportions.

So for the moment, the wolves of Isle Royale are safe. They represent a tiny fragment of the rich heritage the red men held in trust for us over the millennia. In pondering the story of the wolves of Isle Royale, we catch a brief glimpse of past splendor. Yet it could all end as suddenly and as unexpectedly as it began. The wolves could leave the island the same way they came, crossing the ice one winter's day and returning to the mainland, there to face their fate from poison, snare, trap, and gun. On at least one occasion in the past, they were observed journeying away from the island, only to turn back when several miles from shore. Maybe some wolves have left, making the crossing unobserved, and this would explain how the population has managed to remain stable. One day the whole pack may set out, never to return.

What of the moose herd then? Death from starvation and disease awaits them, and although man might possibly be able to control their numbers, he cannot hope to be as discerning as the wolves in weeding out the weak from the strong. He might possibly introduce more wolves, if any are available, but, by that time, it might be too late, the delicate balance lost. Then another brief chapter in the saga of the Northlands will be closed.

6

The Engineers

It was the hour of the dawn, and a soft, diffused light shone pale gray over the island as it lay shrouded in mist. Clouds veiled the shadowy tops of the pines and beads of moisture silvered every twig and leaf and fern. No wind stirred to sweep away the smoking wraiths of vapor, and in the stillness, the scolding of a squirrel split the silence like a whiplash.

A little way from the campsite, the trail swung to the left, following the banks of a stream. Dense thickets of low bushes hid the water from view, but a soft, splashing sound betrayed the presence of life. It might have been a fish or a diving bird, but it sounded as though it was made by something more substantial. I stepped off the trail and moved softly through the bushes, parting them and peering through until I could get a clear view of the stream.

In front of me was a tangled heap of sticks, like an accumulation of driftwood washed down in a flood. Yet the sticks looked too new and green to have been cut any length of time, and some of them had been entirely stripped of their bark. Suddenly, I realized that what I was looking at was no mere pile of driftwood, but a beaver lodge.

As I watched, there came the faint splashing again, and a soft, mewing wail that was almost human in tone. Widening ripples spread across the water, and a small head came into view. The beaver swam toward the lodge, hugging the bank of the stream. It reached the base of the lodge, paused, and then emerged, a portly, dripping figure that clambered laboriously up the mound of sticks bearing a great load of mud, which it held clasped under its chin with its forepaws. It flopped its burden onto the roof of the lodge with an audible grunt of relief, and turning, made its way with great deliberation down the steep side of the lodge and back into the water.

Another beaver appeared, towing a section of log which it added to the pile that formed the lodge, dropping it haphazardly into place and swimming away without a backward glance. Then two more beavers arrived, although whether they were the same pair or not I had no means of telling. They had joined forces to bring a longer length of tree trunk, and together they maneuvered the unwieldly object up river and into position. All the while, they called to each other, and it was impossible to believe that they weren't conversing, although whether they were encouraging each other, or giving instructions or advice, I had no way of knowing. Certainly I could detect no note of dissension.

A loud, rasping noise came from the bank under my feet. Two small beaver were busy stripping the bark off a log, rotating it with their forepaws, and snipping up the torn shreds of bark with their enormous orange incisors. Breakfast over, the log, now gleaming white, was added to the pile on the lodge, and the beaver slipped away downstream once more.

I watched until the sun dissolved away the mist, until I heard the voices of early rising campers echoing along the trail. The beaver heard them too. There was a resounding splash as one hit the water with its broad, flat tail, and next moment, the little people of the stream had vanished.

Here was the architect who would shape the future form of Isle Royale, carving his signature on the landscape as his forebears had done over the centuries. For beavers have made the North woods what they are today, and in so doing have decreed the destinies of all other forms of life, including man.

A stream flows through the forest, its waters hidden from the sun, its banks crowded by a dense growth of willow and aspen, poplar, birch, and alder, with here and there a solitary balsam and jack pine. In the swift, cold current of the stream, a few small trout snatch a precarious living from the airborne insects that fall from the trees, and an occasional mink harries the fish as it journeys upstream from one lake to another.

One spring, after the ice and snows have melted, a pair of beavers make their way upstream. They find the food to their liking, linger, and decide to stay.

Before long, the stream is blocked by a dam of sticks, stones, and mud, and as the water level rises, more materials are added to the dam. Working stealthily, and mainly by night, the beavers cut down trees with their sharp incisor teeth and maneuver the poles into position. Much of the bark, the smaller twigs, and the fresh green leaves are eaten, but as the short summer passes and the first frosts begin to paint the leaves, the beaver begin to lay in a winter store of food—a vast tangle of twigs and branches, sunk below the surface of the water, where the frost cannot reach it.

Meanwhile, they have built their lodge, a mound of branches hollowed out in the center, with the entrance under water. The mound is plastered with mud, which the beaver scoop from the soft ground at the margins of the rising lake. As time passes, the beavers gradually cut channels, radiating out from the pond into the woodland, narrow canals down which they can float long lengths of wood. Where necessary, the beaver dam these canals to maintain a sufficient depth of water.

The years pass, and where once the forest crowded down to the stream, cutting out light and warmth from the earth, there is now a broad lake. A few dead pines still stand, black and stark above the water, and provide convenient perches for an osprey, a kingfisher, or perhaps even an eagle.

The warm, placid waters of the pond are enriched with minerals dissolved from the flooded floor of the forest and further fertilized with the droppings of the beaver. Now microscopic life springs to bloom, to feed a host of tiny creatures which are called, collectively, the zooplankton. Higher plants, lilies, and pondweed, take root in the mud, and soon aquatic insects and fish arrive. Bass lie in ambush in the shadows of sunken logs. Sunfish swim in shoals. A turtle lies in the mud.

Water lilies star the surface of the lake, and a mallard duck leads her brood nervously out of the shelter of the horsetails. The passage of the ducklings is noted by a waiting pike. Muskrats make their nests in the margins of the pond, and at sunset, a moose lurches out from the woods and wades into deep water to browse on the lily stems.

The seasons change. In the winter, the beavers lie snug beneath their thatch, insulated from the cold and protected by a layer of frozen mud and branches so thick and so solidly woven together that it would take a charge of dynamite to break it apart. In the spring, the parents are joined by the young that have been born in the lodge and are now eager for a taste of fresh green food. So the good work goes on, and the engineering and the mining, the navigating, the woodcutting, and the timber-hauling proceed apace.

Such a situation cannot continue indefinitely. By his own industry, the beaver so radically alters the environment on which he depends, that he exhausts his food supplies. Sometimes fate intervenes. Sometimes famine claims him as a victim, for occasionally an exceptionally severe winter will linger on into a late spring and, trapped beneath the ice, the beaver eats the last of his winter store, weeks before the warm winds and rain come to liberate him.

During most years, the beaver colonies grow in numbers and in size. As the supplies of preferred food diminish, the beaver is forced to wander further afield, deserting the security of his pond and traveling overland in search of suitable trees. At such times, especially in early spring, when they are ravenous for fresh food, the beaver fall an easy prey to the wolf.

The beaver is a substantial rodent. Except for the capybara, he is the largest of his tribe. Beavers never stop growing, and an old adult may well top forty pounds in weight. On Isle Royale, they make up about ten per cent of the diet of the wolf, and probably fill an important gap in spring when yearling moose calves are fleet and hard to catch, and the calves of summer are yet to be born.

In the latter part of the last century, trappers exterminated the beaver of Isle Royale. By the 1920's they had begun to make a slow comeback, but trapping kept the population low. Then the island became a national park, and in the decade that followed, beaver colonies erupted into every lake and stream. When the wolves arrived, there were signs that the beavers were close to exhausting their food supplies, but the wolves took control, and the beavers, though still common, are not now abundant.

After death has visited the beaver colony, the deserted dam lies rotting in the sun and grass grows on the roof of the lodge. As the slow forces of decay go to work, the dam crumbles, and the waters of the lake gradually sink and drain away. Where the heron once fished and waded in the sunlit shallows, he now stalks through tall marsh grasses, hunting frogs and small snakes. Soon he will be pouncing on mice and voles as they run their burrows through the carpet of dry moss and reeds.

In the rich silt left behind by the lake, many seeds take

root, among them those of the softwood trees that first attracted the beaver. In the shelter and the sunlight, the new vegetation grows fast and attracts a host of small creatures, squirrels and mice, and snowshoe hares. Birds come too, to nest
and to feed, and in their turn, the predators—fox, weasel, and
mink. Then come the moose, and last, to dine at the table
which, by killing the beaver, he has unwittingly laid, comes
the wolf.

In time, the forest reclaims its own. And in time, the
beaver will return to start again the old, slow cycle, conserving
water, letting in sunlight, enriching the forest floor, and pre-
paring a banquet for a host of other creatures, each of which
complements the lives of others. Without them, the forest
would become a lonely shrine to the trees, ill-lit and peopled
only by squirrels and passing gray jays.

In the years to come, the beavers of Isle Royale may help
to slow the growth of the forest toward climax, that maturity
of the North woods when the trees reign supreme, when their
giant crowns throw a dense canopy of shade over the forest
floor—a gloom so dark that nothing else can grow. In the summer, the beaver ponds will provide rich grazing beds of water
lilies and weeds, and the new growth of willow and aspen in
the old meadows will prove a valuable source of winter browse
for the moose. Over the passage of time, the beavers will play
their part in the slow and patient process of building soil, the
earth that is the womb of the wilderness.

7

The Wolf Pack at Large

Some two decades after their arrival, the wolf packs of Isle Royale became the most thoroughly documented in history, when Durward L. Allen, Professor of Wildlife Ecology at Purdue University, arranged with the National Parks Service to carry out a study of the wolves and their prey. The man chosen for the task was L. David Mech, then a senior wildlife student at Cornell.

During the next three years, Mech set a standard for research in the field which many have since tried to emulate but few could hope to better. He spent sixty-five weeks camping on the island, during which time he hiked over one thousand four hundred miles along the trails, and, piloted by Don Murray, flew over four hundred hours on aerial surveys. His thesis earned him his doctorate, and it was later published as a monograph entitled *The Wolves of Isle Royale*.

From the air, Mech was able to follow the wolf packs on their hunting expeditions and to witness the drama of the kill. His field notes, reproduced in the monograph, describe in stark, vivid detail the last moments in the life of a moose and the violent struggles that often ensue before the wolves can overwhelm their victim.

In every case, the wolves launched their attack on the moose by slashing and worrying at its rump. No attempt was made to hamstring the victim, the aim was rather to inflict massive damage to the muscles of the thighs, in order to slow down the moose and cripple it. The heavy bleeding that followed such injuries further weakened and exhausted the prey until it could no longer stand, whereupon the wolf pack would close in, snapping and biting at nose, throat, face, and flanks.

Sometimes the end was mercifully swift. A nine-month-old calf was dispatched in five minutes, and, after a short chase, a cow was killed in ten minutes. Frequently, however, the wolves are reluctant or unable to press home their initial attack, and the wounded moose will linger for hours, its wounds slowly stiffening and its life ebbing away. All around, the wolf pack waits, licking the bloodstains from the snow or lying at ease on the ice. On occasion, the pack will abandon a wounded moose and move away to make a fresh kill, only to return a day or so later to finish off the cripple, or, if it has succumbed to its wounds, to scent out the carcass.

Wolves invariably have to endure a fair amount of rough handling during an attack on a moose. Often, it is only the yielding softness of the snow that saves a wolf from certain death. A wounded animal will charge through a thicket, dragging the wolves that cling to its rump and flanks behind it. Frequently, a wolf will seize a moose by its nose, thus preoccupying it while other members of the pack attack its rump. The nose wolf hangs on, flying through the air as the moose shakes its head in an effort to dislodge it.

To cut through to the rump of a moose, the wolf has to bite through five inches of hair and hide. The canine teeth are longer and sharper, and the bite of the wolf more powerful and terrible than that of any dog. In comparison with a German shepherd, the face of the wolf when viewed from the front is seen to be fuller and rounder in the cheeks. This is because the temporal and masseter muscles, which provide the motive power for the bite, are more massive in the wolf than in the dog.

Strength and speed are vital to the wolf in attacking a moose—strength to hang on, and speed to launch the assault and also to dodge the flying hooves of the quarry. Deep snow often hampers the wolf, slowing him down during the chase, and reducing the strength of his spring as he leaps to attack. Even worse is snow which has frozen to a thin, hard cust which is not strong enough to support his weight. Then with each stride the wolf breaks through, and the sharp ice gashes his forelegs. A slightly thicker crust, however, is to the wolf's advantage, for then he can run on the surface, while the moose breaks through, injuring its legs. In such conditions moose are especially vulnerable, for they tend to yard in cedar swamps, tramping out a corral of flattened snow on which they can move freely but from which they find it difficult to escape.

Yet in spite of its speed and strength, the wolf has a very low rate of success in hunting moose. In seventy-seven attempts observed by Mech, the wolves killed only six animals. The other seventy-one either ran away or stood their ground so effectively that the wolf pack was intimidated from attacking further. This gives the wolf, as a predator, a success rate of slightly less than eight per cent.

Such a success rate seems ridiculously low when compared with human endeavor. The marksman who hit the target eight times in every hundred shots would either give up shooting or go mad. But undeterred by repeated failure, the wolf moves on, and survives. In fact, the success rate of Isle Royale wolves is on a par with that discovered for wolves elsewhere, and indeed, compares very favorably with the success rate of other predators.

It must be remembered too that the initial chase by the wolves is not an attempt to kill, but merely a test to assess the victim's potential strength and speed. Yet the wolf's skill in judging is difficult to gauge, for Mech records seven occasions where moose were wounded but not killed. What may never be determined is the number of moose the wolves might have killed or injured had they been more vigorous and determined in their initial attack.

All the same, it would seem that the wolf's judgment is fairly well balanced, erring neither too far on the side of caution nor proving too rash or foolhardy. Aggressive action on the part of cow moose undoubtedly thwarts attacks by wolves on several calves, and soft snow, too, hampers the pack on occasions.

There can be no doubt that wolves have a healthy respect for the speed and strength of their prey. Indeed, an enraged and healthy moose is an awesome spectacle. With ears flattened and mane erect, the angry moose extends its neck and holds its head low, retracting its lips and repeatedly protruding its tongue to lick its nose. The sharp, cloven hooves, fore and hind, lash out in all directions with great speed and accuracy. Often the moose rears up onto its hind legs, its forelegs pawing the air as a prelude to stamping its enemy into the snow. A cow will repeatedly charge in defense of her calf, often to good effect, demoralizing the pack so that it flees, or distracting the wolves until the calf can make good its escape.

Respect for the moose may be one reason why the main wolf pack on Isle Royale is so large, for fifteen members is above average in numbers for a pack. Perhaps more moose are intimidated into running by the appearance of so many wolves, for certainly it is impossible for every member to attack at once. There simply isn't enough room on the moose! Usually, seven or eight wolves lead the attack, the others following behind and later taking turns at harassing the victim.

Nor is the carcass of a moose large enough to permit the entire pack to feed at once. Invariably, two or three have to wait until others have eaten their fill. The pack gorges for the first few hours, consuming anything up to twenty pounds of meat apiece, before curling up close to the kill and going to sleep. After a short nap, the wolves feed again before seeking a sheltered spot, preferably in the sun, for a more prolonged sleep. This time, several hours may pass before the wolves attempt to feed again, by which time little is left but the skeleton of the moose.

The following day is usually passed in leisurely relaxation, after which the wolves return to the skeleton to spend hours chewing and gnawing at the bones. Calves are consumed entirely. All that may be left of a cow moose is the cleaned skeleton, scattered and pulled apart, with the bones well chewed. The skeleton of a bull may be left intact, but thoroughly stripped of flesh.

Throughout the feast, a flock of ravens wait in nearby trees, and the moment the wolf pack leaves the carcass, the birds glide down to dine. These birds habitually keep pace with the wolf packs, flying ahead of them on their hunting forays and waiting, perched in the trees, for the pack to pass below before flying on again. The ravens wait in evident anticipation as the wolves go in to kill, at times flying around the wounded moose and calling excitedly. It would seem that in wintertime, the ravens of Isle Royale are almost entirely dependent on the wolves for food.

Ravens and wolves appear to enjoy an amicable relationship, and when the wolves are resting after a kill, the ravens tease the wolves, diving on them, and on at least one occasion that Mech observed, pulling their tails. In turn, the wolves stalk the ravens, leaping at them as they fly just above their heads, but either the ravens are very good judges of the distance a wolf can leap, or else the wolves do not try very hard, for no raven ever seems to get caught.

After two or three days, when the carcass is all gone and the pack has slept off the effects of its gargantuan meal, certain wolves begin to show signs of restlessness and a desire to travel again. It is at such times that the wolves may enjoy a group howl.

As yet, no one fully understands the significance of howling. It may be a manifestation of restlessness or frustration, or vocal evidence of some other emotion. It may serve some practical purpose in establishing territory or in assisting in the assembly of a widely scattered pack. Howling may be stimulated by other noises—including sounds made by humans—or it may begin quite spontaneously.

Contrary to popular belief, wolves do not howl to the moon, nor do they only howl in winter. Wolves may howl at any time of the year, at dusk or dawn, at dead of night, or at midday. One thing is certain, however, and that is that wolves love to howl. Some more than others, perhaps, but for each and every member of the pack, it becomes a joyous social occasion, with wolves gathering from all sides, anxious to make contact with each other, flank pressed close to flank. Excitement is evident as each wolf joins the chorus—trembling, eager, bright-eyed, anxious not to miss a moment of the fun.

Duration of the whole chorus varies but usually does not last more than a few minutes. The range of notes is wide, from a deep, melancholy moan to a high-pitched yelp; at times, strongly harmonious chords are struck. It would seem that wolves admire these chords as much as humans, for they hold the notes as long as possible.

As suddenly as it begins, the howling stops. By now, the whole pack is wide-awake and ready for action. After a few moments of aimless and indecisive milling about, the wolves move off in single file behind their leader. Once more, they have reverted to their role of silent killers of the Northlands, slipping through the stillness of a summer night like gray cloud shadows over the face of the moon, or padding tirelessly across the frozen snow, their shadows black in the brilliant glare of the winter sun. Their lives are one long journey, a circle without end.

8

An Island Out of Time

I followed the trail through the forest, now climbing steeply to top a small ridge, now dropping down to cross a narrow valley or the wide, flat expanse of an old deserted beaver meadow. Each turn of the trail showed a different face of the North woods as every shrub and plant and tree grew in response to the laws of light and shade, of temperature and humidity, and depth of soil. Tall stands of maple towered above a breast-high carpet of scrub poplar, clumps of stately aspen rubbed shoulders with the graceful paper birch. Pines stood somber and dark, like hooded monks absorbed in some silent, secret ritual—acolytes of the wild.

So I came to the treeless summit of Mount Ojibway, to stand and look north across the blue haze of Lake Superior and beyond, over Canada, to where there was no horizon, only the blue of the land, fading imperceptibly to merge with the great, empty vault of the sky. The wind blew cold and clean, and the air had a freshness and purity unchanged since the passing of the Ice Age. I was aware of an intense desire to be free, to shed my physical shell and drift unimpeded over that awful immensity of landscape—across the lakes and forests and foaming rivers—until I came to the tundra and the barren lands, and at last, to the regions of eternal ice and snow. It would be like taking a journey back through time.

Below me, the island—its trees and wooded hills—lay billowed out like a discarded cloak of mossy green velvet in whose folds lakes nestled like jewels spilled from a rich man's purse and sparkling in the yellow light of the sun. It lay as it had lain since before the coming of the white man, before the arrival of the first Indians, as it will lay until the coming of a new Ice Age, when the snows will fall without ceasing and the great glaciers will rumble and groan again across a frozen continent. Until then, it will endure.

From where I stood, I could survey the entire island, and I knew that somewhere, lost among the trees and the hollows of the hills, were a few hundred moose and a handful of wolves. I knew, too, that in weight and numbers the moose and the wolves and the pine trees were of little significance when compared to the greater mass of life on the island. For there was life all around—life in the water and in the soil, life in the decaying stumps of the trees, life borne on the wind and fermenting in the rotting fruit of the berry bushes, life in forms too small to be visible to the naked eye. Yet it was there, in such astronomical numbers and such diversity of form as to be beyond comprehension.

The environment was like a giant supermarket, an enterprise which had grown out of a policy of small profits and rapid turnover, and this had proved so successful that there was no room for further expansion. Every shelf, every nook and cranny in the store was crammed to bursting point with goods and, as fast as the stocks were sold, they were replaced. Turnover, in fact, was so rapid that there was no time for stock taking, for even if lists were to be prepared, the pattern would have changed before the counting was complete.

Meanwhile, the profits were mounting; and so, rather than let capital lie idle, the environment turned to long-term investment—to moose and wolves and pine trees—to securities that could be expected to mature in ten, or fifteen, or a hundred years' time, yet still be cashed in at any given moment.

For the environment is cautious and frugal in its long-term investments and ever mindful of its original formula for success. So when disaster strikes in the form of flood, or fire, or drought, these assets are the first to be realized in terms of environmental cash, and for awhile, the supermarket of the wild goes back to its old way of trading.

Any habitat, however inhospitable it might appear to man, however delicately it might be balanced, must have accumulated a fair degree of wealth to support such mammals as moose and wolves. Viewed in isolation, the existence of such beasts seems pointless and trivial, even in relationship to the vegetation of Isle Royale. The presence or absence of wolves and moose might alter the pattern of growth, might change it radically. Nothing could totally destroy it.

However long they coexisted, the moose and wolves were assured of but a brief sojourn on the island for, although the pendulum of the evolutionary clock swings slow, the clock never stops, and in evolutionary time, the existence of both mammals has been so brief as to be almost unmarked on the dial of destiny.

Yet it seemed to me that if the rest of the environment permitted them to survive, then the wolf and the moose were important to the rest of the living world. Each species served the environment in its way. It played its role and received the reward of life. Wolf and moose and man were fellow travelers from the Pleistocene epoch, brother mammals whose antecedents had each emerged to make his own way out of the primordial mud of creation. There is no evidence to suggest that the journey is over.

Already, over fifteen million years have rolled by since tomarctus—the ancestor of wolves, dogs, and foxes—stalked the earth on his short, squat legs. At that time, a primitive, anthropoid ape called proconsul was proving so successful as a species that his numbers were spreading out from central Africa to Asia and Europe. Doubtless the paths of proconsul and tomarctus crossed.

As the savage Miocene droughts mellowed into the more temperate climate of the Pliocene, an upright anthropoid emerged to roam the plains in small bands, a carnivorous ape who had learned to hunt herbivores and to augment his strength with a club of bone. So, long before true man appeared out of the mists of the Pleistocene, before the dire wolf hunted the camelops and the giant beaver of that epoch, the evolutionary paths of wolf and man were on a collision course.

Slowly, inexorably, two totally differing mammalian species converged along their separate pathways to inhabit the same terrain, to hunt in the same way, to eat the same food, to compete for survival. Long before man learned to till the fields, long before he began to herd flocks, he must have grown to hate the wolf. The roots of man's enmity toward the wolf lie buried deep, and all the folklore and fable, all the songs and ballads, and Biblical references serve only to nourish those roots.

The human instinctively fears the wolf, and stories such as *Little Red Riding Hood, Peter and the Wolf,* and *The Three Little Pigs* are the result of that fear, not the cause. Such fear is not born anew in each innocent child. It is already there, ingrained, and legend serves merely to enforce it.

The seeds of hatred were sown, yet neither the enmity of one animal species toward another nor the natural antipathy aroused in man by the presence of a dangerous predator is sufficient in itself to explain the illogical terror, the almost pathological dread, that, in the past, the wolf has inspired in man.

True, the wolf seems tailor-made of the stuff from which ghost stories are woven. He is gray, a creature of the twilight, with slant eyes and a voice that at times can be uncannily human. His role as scavenger, on battlefields and in villages where plague or smallpox has struck, has helped to promote his ghoulish nature. Still the essential evidence, that which brands the wolf as the epitome of evil, is lacking.

The first European settlers in the New World were already deeply imbued with wolf lore and legend. Even their Bible spoke of false prophets dressed in sheeps' clothing, who were, in reality, "ravening wolves." The Germans believed that the devil squatted between the beast's eyes, and the Finns maintained that unbaptized children wandered the earth in the form of wolves. The French were, and still are, terrified of wolves, and when, in 1963, it was thought that a small pack was at large in France, the news made international headlines.

From time immemorial, wolves have been associated with witchcraft. The Latin term "lupulla," or "little wolf," means witch, or a woman of easy virtue. Romulus and Remus, who were reputed to have been suckled by a she-wolf, were probably the offspring of a prostitute. In Germany, witches were said to ride wolves, and in Lorraine, the "witchmaster" turned into a wolf to go to the witches' sabbath.

This belief, that men and women could metamorphose into wolves, was widespread and reinforced during the dark ages of medieval superstition. A thin shred of truth supports the legend, for there is an incurable mental illness, fortunately rare, known as lycanthropy, in which the victim develops a taste for raw or putrid meat, a desire to run naked through the woods, and sometimes, an urge to rape and kill. There was, too, a higher incidence of leprosy in the Middle Ages than occurs today, and this disease, in its leonine form, often gave the victim the features of a wild beast.

Even so, the belief in werewolfism, in all its nightmarish

detail, is perhaps too strong to be explained away by disease or insanity. Perhaps we have to go back farther in time, to an era when man was still evolving, to a period when a gentle, intelligent humanoid, a peaceful vegetarian, suffered from continued attacks and assaults from an aggressive, carnivorous humanoid, either excessively hirsute, or clad in the skins of animals. Such clashes could leave a collective scar on the unconscious minds of a peace-loving people.

If the two species were genetically compatible, the consequences of such an assault could leave more than scars. Perhaps *Homo sapiens* is such a hybrid, a dual personality, forever in conflict with himself. Man, the gentle, merciful creator, is continually being driven down by the beast within him.

As Lord Byron wrote:

> Lycanthropy
> I comprehend, for without transformation,
> Men become wolves on any slight occasion.

So perhaps, even today, when man meets wolf, he sees before him a mirror image of his worst enemy, one from whom there can be no escape.

The wolf, for his part, fears and distrusts man and evinces this fear by keeping out of the way. Such behavior serves to heighten enmity, to widen the gap of understanding. Tomarctus gave us many sons. One was *canis familiaris,* the domestic dog, who came to live with man, to share his table and his fire. In turn, he became servant, protector, and court jester and so earned the dubious title of "man's best friend."

Another son, *canis lupus,* the wolf, would have nothing to do with man. Even wolves raised in captivity and shown every kindness remain timid and fearful, although capable of affection for their owners. Early man must have been quick to notice the difference in temperament between wolf and fireside dog, and perhaps rationalized this difference by coming to the conclusion that the wolf must be evil.

The pathway from the Pleistocene has been arduous and long, but the end of the trail is not yet in sight. Man and moose and wolf and dog have survived, each in his own way, yet who can foretell what changes the world will witness in the millennia still to come?

The sun was westering as I set off down the mountain. I was about to leave Isle Royale. Before I had landed on the island, I knew that regulations were designed to keep me on the move, to cause me to have as little impact on the environment as possible. The authorities now devoted what energies they had left, and these were not inconsiderable, in trying to persuade me to leave. It was not that anyone was in any way discourteous or unhelpful. Without exception, the staff was considerate and polite. Yet the hidden implication was clear. Neither I, nor anyone else, was wanted on Isle Royale.

Nor was it because it was the end of the season, although the staff were packing up so fast it made my head spin. The truth was that man was not wanted in an environment where his status could not be other than that of a pest. Although this was never put into words, it was obvious; and although at first the realization came as a considerable blow to my ego, I later came to have a deep respect for the policy. As I moved about the island, it was clear that although the vacation period was short and the number of visitors few in comparison to other national parks, man had by sheer weight of numbers caused significant damage.

Around the official campsites fallen timber was scarce, and the ground in front of the wooden leanto shelters was worn bare. The passage of booted feet had turned the trails into deep ruts to a point where some had had to be closed to give the environment time to repair itself.

There were, too, other dangers inherent in man's presence

on the island. At anytime, a moment's carelessness with a match could start a forest fire which would sweep unchecked across the island unless the wardens could get it under control. Other fears, too, must have plagued the minds of the staff and added to the weight of their responsibility. Someone might break a limb, go down with any one of a dozen contagious diseases, or develop acute appendicitis. In addition to the risk of sickness among the human population, there was the ever-present fear of an epidemic of distemper or contagious jaundice among the wolf packs.

There was a boat leaving for the mainland in the morning. Unless I wished to spend another week on the island, I had to be aboard. The previous evening, I had talked with a man who was familiar with the canoe country of the Superior National Forest, in northern Minnesota. I decided I would journey there to seek out the canoe outfitters he had mentioned, and from there, make my way into the vast wilderness that lay sprawled on both sides of the Canadian border. There, perhaps, I might find the wolves that had eluded me on Isle Royale.

In the clear light of early dawn, I stood on the stern of the launch and watched as the forest wall slid by. As always, the pines stood in ritual silence; yet, their presence no longer seemed as hostile as it had at first. I knew, as I bid them a wordless farewell, that without them, without the moose and the wolves and the beaver, Isle Royale would cease to live.

9

Wolf Society

The motor vessel *Ranger III* takes six hours to make the journey across Lake Superior from Isle Royale to the mainland of Michigan. I stared out over the tumbling blue waste of white-capped waves, devoid of any life save for an occasional wandering gull or the dark, squat bulk of a giant ore carrier, plowing across from Duluth toward the Gulf of St. Lawrence, and I began to get some idea of the immensity of this, the largest body of fresh water in the world.

For the moment, I was utterly dependent on an artificial life support system, created and constructed by that most fallible of creatures, my fellow-man. If the boat were to sink, how long, I wondered, would I last in those ice-cold waters? Would I be able to swim, or would cold and cramp knot my limbs and paralyze my muscles so that I sank?

It occurred to me that the whole of civilization was fast becoming an artificial life support system, a sort of spaceship from which we humans emerge now and again to explore that alien planet Earth. Even when I go into the wilderness, I take with me the essentials of the life support system on which I am

most dependent—tent, sleeping bag, cooking utensils and a knife, the means of making fire, and a store of dehydrated foods. When my food supplies are gone, I must return to civilization or run the risk of starving.

Could man survive the collapse of that life support system on which he has become dependent? Alone and unarmed, he would be reduced to the status of a root-grubbing ape, berry picking, fruit gathering, and dependent for his protein on the smallest and weakest members of the animal kingdom— nestling birds and baby mice, the larvae of beetles and moths, anything that was too slow or too feeble to avoid capture.

As a member of a group, man's chances of survival would be infinitely greater, for the group would emerge as a loose-knit, cooperative band, roaming the plains and wooded hills, armed with sticks and stones and sharpened bones. Any game sighted would be chased and harried, cornered and trapped, until it could be stabbed, and bludgeoned, and stoned to death.

For this is how we began, and this is how we lived down through countless millennia until a mere ten thousand years ago, and those instincts which today, from the security of our present way of life, we tend to regard as base and primitive, are those which ensured our survival. We have not lost them, and although we ignore them, they have not begun to weaken. The climb up from the Pleistocene has been arduous and long, but the way back is slippery and steep.

The actual killing of the quarry would be messy and slow, especially if the victim was large. Yet it would be in our interests to go for big game, for one kill would ensure an equal share out among the group and guarantee several days' supply of food before it went bad. In other words, we would function and behave exactly like a wolf pack.

The way of the pack is deeply engrained in wolf instinct. Most authorities are agreed that the pack is basically a family unit made up of a mated couple, and their one- or two-year-old offspring. Sometimes two families will band together, at least for awhile; here again, there is probably some kinship between the respective pack leaders. A wolf pack may consist then of four to ten members, although larger groups have been recorded. In the past, packs of between twenty and thirty wolves have been reported from Minnesota and Alaska.

There are one or two authenticated records of wolf packs in Alaska numbering up to fifty members. Such a pack would be a formidable army indeed, and it is doubtful if larger packs ever existed anywhere in the world. Certainly, accounts by such writers as Alexandre Dumas, of wolf packs numbering two or three thousand, inhabiting the treeless deserts of Russia, can be dismissed as so much science fiction.

All the same, the wolf is a social animal, and the wolf pack is strongest—most closely knit—in winter, when game is harder to catch and the young wolves are strong and tireless. For in addition to being gregarious, the wolf has another inherent trait: He is born to wander. So the pack ranges over a wide territory, traveling for half the day at a tireless trot. This territory the pack claims as its own, marking the boundaries with scent from their anal glands and strategically placed drops of urine. They further proclaim their proprietory rights by howling, and so each pack keeps its neighbors informed of its presence, identity, and numbers.

A strong pack demands a strong leader, and this leader, known as the alpha male, is dominant over every other wolf in the pack. This dominance is maintained by constant warning barks and growls, the baring of teeth, and a number of facial expressions which are themselves part of a body language. Approach, gait, stance, the angle of the head and tail to the body, the way in which the tail is waved or wagged, every gesture on the part of a wolf is meaningful to others in the pack.

Each wolf is aware of its social standing in the hierarchy of the pack—being dominant to some and subservient to others, down to the smallest, weakest member, who is subservient to all. Any observer, however, who tries to work out the hierarchy of a pack, usually retires baffled with a book full of incomprehensible notes, partly because the body language of wolves is so complex, and partly because the wolves are so perceptive and observant, so quick to see the signs, that the observer misses the signal or fails to note that it has been given at all. The situation is further complicated by the fact that if a dispute breaks out, the quarrel is never allowed to remain a private one; the whole pack joins in. Such disputes are rare, however, and the system tends to lead to a rough harmony within the pack. Dominance is maintained without the need for rending fangs and bloodshed.

Throughout the winter, the pack hunts, and kills, and sleeps curled up in hollows in the snow. The breeding season occurs during the period from mid-February to mid-March, but although the mating of the alpha male and female is a pretty public affair, much of the private life of the wolf remains a mystery.

Male wolves mature in three years and females in two. Where mating occurs between pack members other than the leaders, the pack probably comprises more than one family. Other times, there seems to be some inhibitory force at work which prevents wolves other than the dominant pair from mating. Perhaps the males are simply too young, or maybe they are repressed by the alpha male. Young females in breeding condition must meet up with young males from other packs, and indeed, tracks in the snow at this time of the year suggest that many a pair is on honeymoon.

The gestation period lasts about nine weeks, and toward the end of this time, the she-wolf leaves the pack, either to dig a den or to refurbish one with which she is familiar. Here the cubs, weighing about a pound apiece, are born—deaf, blind, and helpless. There may be as many as seven or eight in a litter, but probably three or four is the more usual number.

The cubs grow fast. In ten to fourteen days, their eyes open, their legs, which at first were too weak to support their weight, grow longer and stronger, as the exercise of feeding from their mother develops their muscles. Soon they are rolling and tumbling toward the mouth of the den. About this time, the mother elects to move them to a fresh denning area where there is room for the cubs to play outside and there is water for them to drink as they are weaned.

Until now, the father has remained away from his cubs, hunting with the remainder of the pack while continuing to maintain contact with the mother. Now he brings the cubs meat, either in his mouth or in his stomach. On arrival at the den, the cubs crowd around, welcoming him and begging him to regurgitate the food. This practice of regurgitation, though slighly repellent to man, at least insures that the meat is kept clean and warm on its journey, and makes traveling easier for the wolf.

About this time, too, other members of the pack visit the den, and from time to time, the mother will leave her young in charge of a baby-sitter, or sitters, while she goes off hunting. Few wolf cubs are short of a number of uncles and aunts, for all wolves love cubs and display endless tolerance and patience in enduring hours of torment from teeth, claws, and the impact of sturdy little bodies.

Such attentiveness on the part of the older wolves is invaluable to the youngsters for, during this period, the cubs not only develop their muscles with wrestling bouts and interminable games of tag and tug of war, but they also learn the social graces, the body language of wolves. So, right from the start, the young wolf takes his part in society, grows acquainted with his relations, and identifies with the pack.

If all goes well, by the end of the summer the young wolf

weighs up to sixty pounds and is strong enough to survive the rigorous testing of his first winter. As the geese call out across the sky, as the ice crackles along the margins of the lakes, and the golden leaves of the birches glow like candles on the hills, the pack draws closer together, united by a common bond.

Already the young have made numerous expeditions away from the den in the company of their parents or other members of the pack. Throughout the warm, scented nights of summer, they have followed the chase, been in at the kill, and taken their share of the feast. Now they have forsaken the den altogether, and from now on, they will sleep out in the open beneath the stars or under the shading canopy of the trees. Even in subzero temperatures, they will sleep snug in the snow, sheltered from the icy wind, and protected from the frost by the luxurious warmth of their fur. Curled tight into balls, their tails covering their noses and their pads tucked close to their bodies, they are immune to cold.

When the pack kills, the young wolf feeds well, gorging perhaps twenty pounds of meat before falling asleep. In the intervals between kills—periods of time varying from two days to a week or more—the young wolf grows accustomed to going hungry. So the months and years pass, and the wolf grows in skill and strength until one day he may become the leader of his own pack.

Seven years is regarded as the average length of life in the wild for a wolf. Some wolves ten years old may still be in their prime, but by the time twelve or fourteen years are reached, the wolf is worn and old, his teeth reduced to broken stumps, and his legs lame from countless bites and bruises. No longer able to run with the pack, perhaps even driven from it by younger, stronger males, the wolf wanders alone, feeding from carrion and abandoned kills, subsisting on berries and roots or such small game as he can capture.

Wolf history abounds with stories and legends about lone

wolves so that they have acquired a certain mystique. Although lone wolves do occur as a natural phenomenon, I suspect that during the day of the wolfhunter, many were made lone. Trappers agreed that young wolves were usually easy to catch, but that their parents were more elusive. Often it happened that a litter would be dug out, and the female shot on her return to the den, or the male might be shot while the female escaped. Either way, a wolf was made solitary.

Such a wolf, especially if advanced in years, might well turn to cattle and sheep stealing, and having learned to respect man, would gow increasingly cunning and elusive. In the past, trappers have spent months, even years, in dedicated pursuit of such an individual, and have acquired a deep respect for the wiliness of their quarry.

It may be that in pursuing the lone wolf with such dedication, and eventually bringing about its death, the trapper does his victim a service. Whether this is so or not, it cannot be denied that there is something particularly poignant about the image of a lone wolf, padding over the snow or lifting its muzzle to the stars in a solitary howl. After a lifetime of belonging, of being part of a whole, the days of the lone wolf must be empty indeed.

10

The Pattern of the Forest

From Duluth, the highway runs north and east along the shores of Lake Superior toward the Canadian border. About a hundred miles out along the way lies the little township of Tofte, and from here, the Sawbill Trail reaches out to pierce the heart of the Superior National Forest. It is a primitive road—in winter treacherous with hard-packed snow and ice, in summer dusty when dry and muddy when wet, riddled with deep ruts and bone-jarring potholes. For twenty-four miles, it runs slightly west of north, climbing with many a switchback and hump to a height four hundred feet above the lake and a thousand feet above sea level. All the way along the trail, the green walls of the forest crowd down to its sides.

The forest itself lies sprawled over a vast area, covering some three million acres—over four thousand five hundred square miles—representing a tiny fragment of the great circumpolar forests of the Northern Hemisphere. Here lies the last stronghold of the eastern timber wolf, and here, it seems, he is inviolable. Here he enjoys at least the nominal protection of the law for the purely practical reason that anyone concerned with growing trees is anxious to control those animal populations that might damage growing timber. The wolf is eminently suited to this task, and furthermore, he needs neither a weekly wage nor a rifle and ammunition.

Once he steps off forest land, however, the wolf is fair game and liable to fall victim to trap, and snare, and gun. Furthermore, there is no closed season. Immured within the forest boundaries, can the wolf survive? Can even this vast area support a viable population of wolves?

How many wolves there are in the Superior National Forest nobody seems to know. Indeed, the population is sharply divided into rival factions, those who believe the wolf to be declining in numbers, in danger of becoming extinct in Minnesota, and those who aver that far from being endangered, the wolf is actually on the increase, and threatens to eliminate the stocks of white-tailed deer.

In 1955, Milt Stenlund, a biologist, published results of a survey carried out two years previously, which showed that approximately three to four hundred timber wolves inhabited seven thousand square miles of territory in northern Minnesota. This gave an average density of one wolf for every seventeen square miles. This is a much lower density than the figure of one wolf to ten square miles quoted by David Mech for Isle Royale, especially when it is remembered that the territory of the large pack did not cover the whole island, but only a hundred and five square miles, thus giving a density of one wolf to six-and-a-half square miles.

Stenlund's estimates are now twenty years old, and it is conceivable that wolf densities have altered in the meantime. The Conservation Department, and the Department of Natural Resources estimate that, in 1970, the wolf population ranged from three to five hundred and that today it could be five hundred to a thousand.

Over what area? Here again, the figures are vague, for the

territory inhabited by the wolf in northern Minnesota is variously assessed at anything from twelve to twenty-five thousand miles. Nobody is prepared to say how many wolves live in the Superior National Forest itself.

Some local inhabitants are inclined to doubt official figures. One man puts the present population of wolves in northern Minnesota at between two and three thousand. Others—trappers and loggers—who are reputed to know the country, guess nearer four thousand. David Mech quotes guesses ranging from three hundred to forty thousand.

Counting wolves cannot be easy. In Ontario, biologists and conservation officers spent six years and eight hundred hours of helicopter flying before arriving at an accurate estimate of the wolf population in an area of just over one thousand square miles. Counts of wolf populations over the North American continent, where they have been made, range from a low of one wolf to sixty-eight miles in Alberta to the high count made by David Mech on Isle Royale. There may be seasonal variations, too. In Jasper National Park, it is believed that there is one wolf to every hundred square miles in summer, but that the population increases tenfold in winter!

The more questions I asked, the more confused I became. Since I had no way of knowing, except from hearsay, whether wolf populations were growing or shrinking, I could only make a rough estimate on the figures available. In the end, I arrived at the conclusion that, given a density of one wolf to twenty square miles, the total population would not exceed two hundred and fifty in the Superior National Forest. At the highest density that seemed feasible, one wolf to ten square miles, there might be five hundred wolves. Even though these figures were scarcely close enough to be of value, it showed that estimates of two, three, or four thousand wolves in northern Minnesota were scarcely credible.

Wolf densities over an area of twenty-five thousand square

miles were bound to vary, but to suggest that there were two thousand five hundred wolves in the territory seemed to me to border on the absurd. To achieve an overall density of one wolf to ten square miles over the whole area meant that, in certain places, the wolves would need to be as thick upon the ground as chipmunks round a campsite!

One final complication showed the impossibility of reaching any firm and lasting conclusion regarding wolf population figures. For over a hundred miles, the Superior National Forest marched with the borders of Canada. There was nothing whatever to stop wolves entering or leaving the forest from the north, and no way in which mankind could stem or reverse the flow. For all time, it seemed, the forest would support whatever population of wolves it could tolerate.

Before I got submerged under a tidal wave of contradiction, I decided that I would see for myself this world of the wolf. So it was that on a misty morning in early September, I set out along the Sawbill Trail, and since, technically, the moment I stepped off Highway 61, I was in wolf country, I elected to walk.

Soon I had left behind the untidy huddle of shacks and trailers that bordered the trail, climbing steadily upward, past Tofte dump, with its indigenous population of scavenging brown bears, growing fat and lazy on the leavings of an affluent society. I paused for a moment to look back on the cloud-wreathed majesty of Carlton Peak, rising out of its wooded skirts and rearing skyward like a giant fortress, hued in somber gray and carved from the ancient rocks.

I adjusted my pack and tramped on until all around the living green of the forest encompassed me, seeming to bear down on me with a tangible force, restricting me, holding me back. Mercifully, perhaps, the sun stayed hidden behind a veil of gray cloud, but in the soft, muted light, the somber broadcloth of the forest did nothing to ease my oppression. Once again, as

on Isle Royale, I felt myself defeated, baffled, by the impene-
trability of the forest, and longed for some sign of animal life,
a squarrel, a jay even. For long periods, there was nothing.
There could have been ten thousand wolves dogging my footsteps on either side of the trail.

From time to time, cars or trucks passed, the occupants
staring curiously as they swept by, leaving behind a cloud of
red dust that slowly settled around me. Before long, I began to
regret my decision to follow the Sawbill Trail. Having, liter-
ally, had a taste of the trail, I was anxious to reach the end, for
I was particularly interested in the next stage of my explorations.

Within the forest, like the kernel of a nut, lay the Boundary Waters Canoe Area, the second largest unit of the National
Wilderness Preservation System, and its only canoe area.
Spread across more than a million acres of forest, the BWCA
is a hundred and four miles wide from east to west, and
averages sixteen miles from north to south. At the Canadian
border, it unites with the Quetico National Park of Canada to
form a wilderness area extending over three thousand square
miles.

At first, these figures sounded impressive, but then I
looked at them more closely. The total acreage of the BWCA
is, first of all, divided into three chunks. To the east, the
Gunflint Trail slices off a considerable portion and drives a
nonwilderness corridor through to the Canadian border. Simi-
larly, to the west, the Echo Trail isolates another area. Of the
million acres involved, less than half are designated as a no-
cut zone, and this is in the interior. The remainder, over six
hundred thousand acres, are still subject to the demands and
pressures of commercial forestry.

A look at the map suggests that water occupies more of the
region than does land. This is not so, but at least eighteen per
cent, a hundred and seventy-five thousand acres, are water.

This is fine for the canoeist and the fish, and in many ways of benefit to all the denizens of the forest, but still, in summer at any rate, cuts down the amount of territory available to terrestrial animals.

Each year, from May through September, over one hundred and fifty thousand visitors come to the BWCA, to fish, and camp, and follow the one thousand two hundred miles of canoe routes. Their behavior while in the area is strictly controlled. Entry is by permit only. No one is allowed to stay more than fourteen days in any one site. No bottles or containers are permitted, and no more than ten individuals are allowed in a party. All forms of motorized transport are banned except on a few routes. Even aircraft, except in emergency or on essential forestry business, are banned over the area below a height of four thousand feet.

The very nature of the terrain insures that visitors will be confined to the lakes and waterways, streams and portages. Even so, in spite of every precaution, the presence of so many visitors has a considerable impact on the environment, especially as their influx coincides with the short growing season of one hundred and twenty days. Once again, it seemed, man and wolf were occupying the same ecological niche, and while maybe not competing for food, were utilizing the same space. I looked forward to seeing this natural wilderness for myself, to find out how well it was withstanding the buffeting and bashing of forestry, tourism, and hunting, to see how natural it still was, and how wild.

So I came to the end of the Sawbill Trail, and late one afternoon—for the first time in my life—I stepped gingerly into the stern of a canoe, and grasping the paddle, pushed off. The shoreline slowly receded, the canoe slid gracefully over the surface of the lake, and the paddle sang a soft melody as the great rolling panorama of the North woods slowly unfolded before my eyes. That evening, I camped on a rocky bluff at the end of a short portage, beside a lake whose mirror-calm surface was dimpled by the rings of rising fish. Beyond, the wooded hills rose and fell like the billows of a frozen sea, north toward Canada. Beside my camp, in the soft mud at the edge of the lake, was the clear and unmistakable print of a wolf.

Lumberjacks and Caribou

They came to the North woods, and in the space of half a century, they reaped the harvest of ten thousand years.

Until the mid-nineteenth century, Minnesota contained thirty million acres of virgin timber, thousands of square miles of forest, unbroken save for the occasional fire scar or beaver meadow, largely unexplored, and inhabited only by wandering bands of Chippewa and occasional trappers. This was a land of tall trees—of spruce and fir and tamarack, red pine, and jack pine. Towering above them all grew the white pine.

America was growing fast, forging a civilization out of the raw materials of a continent, and to a nation in desperate need of lumber of all kinds, the white pine was the greatest prize of all. Standing a hundred and twenty feet high, its trunk measuring four, five, or even six feet in diameter at breast height, its timbers were light and strong, straight-grained, and durable. Here in Minnesota, there was, it seemed, an inexhaustible supply of wealth.

The loggers came late to Minnesota, and at first, their numbers were few. Four thousand lumberjacks were at work in

1870, but by the turn of the century, their army was ten times as large. As they moved deeper into the forest, they left behind a wasteland of decaying stumps and abandoned clearings, and across the state, there spread a network of logging roads and railways. The peak year was 1905, when nearly two billion feet of timber were cut, nearly all white pine. Ten years later, the yield was down by half, and by the end of a further decade, it was reduced to a fifth. Shortly after, depression hit the Western world, and anyway, the trees were all gone. There remained a legend, the story of Paul Bunyan, the giant who leveled a section of pine every time he sneezed.

Many people have wondered how it was possible for the loggers to cut over the whole of northern Minnesota in so short a time. Much of the area was lake, or stream, or marshland, and a great deal of the forest was composed of secondary, immature growth. The loggers took only the biggest trees—the best for commercial use—and they cut them, not with axes or with power saws, for these had yet to be invented. Most of the timber was felled with seven-foot crosscut saws.

The average lumber camp consisted of seventy-five to a hundred men. Ten pairs of men were the sawyers, and each pair had a "marker" or notcher, who marked the trees to be felled and measured the fallen timber into logs. Between them, they would harvest from eight to twelve million board feet of timber in a winter season.

The cut logs were skidded out of the woods by teams of horses and oxen, loaded onto sleds, and hauled along specially constructed ice roads. These roads were miracles of planning and construction, and carefully maintained throughout the winter. Remarkable loads could be moved in this way. Perhaps the heaviest was a hundred and forty-four tons of logs hauled by a four-horse hitch along three miles of ice road, en route to the World's Fair exhibition at Chicago in 1893.

It is impossible to assess the loss to the North woods environment brought about by the removal of such an immense volume of timber. Each log hauled represented a holding, a stock investment of mineral and organic wealth, held in bond during the lifetime of the pine, to be returned to the environment upon its death. In less than half a century, this wealth was ripped from the North woods, and its value has never been declared.

Yet the impact of the loggers on the environment was more complex than the mere harvesting of natural wealth. It was state policy at the time to insist on the burning of all the slash and debris left behind in cleared areas, and while to the loggers this was an unnecessary and expensive chore, it released the remaining nutrients—the potash, the phosphates, and other minerals—in a form readily available to plant life. In the light and warmth of the sun, the clearings sprouted a dense growth of browse for game.

To supplement their rations, many logging camps kept herds of pigs, and rations for these—together with oats and hay for the horses and oxen—were hauled into the forests over the tote roads. The spreading of seeds from the hay and the fertility brought to the soil through the droppings of the animals, produced waist-high meadows of timothy and clover.

In the early days of the logging era, game was scarce in the North woods. The loggers were able to buy some meat—moose and deer and caribou—from the Indians, and every camp had its hunter. The lumberjacks could not live off the land, however, and as the industry grew, the men came to expect the best and nothing but the best of food.

Meanwhile, in the cut-over areas, wild game began to increase, so that by the time the first settlers moved in to hack their tiny homesteads out of the wilderness, they found moose and deer, ruffed grouse and pinated grouse, prairie chickens, rabbits, and other game animals in abundance. Since not all the forest had been cut, the game found shelter as well as food. Deer inhabited the cedar swamps, and grouse fed on the aspen stands that had replaced the pines.

Such a bonanza could not be expected to continue indefinitely. As farming increased in intensity, as the state grew more heavily populated, so such game as survived retreated north, and the predators followed. For a long time, the pendulum of change had been swinging wildly, out of control, and even to this day, it still has to settle down. It is difficult to assess, in retrospect, which aspect of the logging era had the greatest impact on the environment—the removal of the long-term wealth or the introduction of instant fertility. It is as if a patient had been bled almost to the point of death and then given massive injections of vitamins and energy boosters to galvanize him into activity.

During this era, one casualty slipped, almost unnoticed and unmourned, into oblivion. For centuries, the North woods had been the territory of a kind of deer known as caribou. Once their legions had been without number. They circumnavigated the North Pole, and it may well have been from Europe, where their cousins the reindeer still survive, that the caribou migrated east across Asia, over the Bering Straits and into the American continent. Perhaps it was these herds that led the red man into America.

The caribou still inhabit the north, in Canada and Alaska, although their numbers have been greatly reduced. Their southern legions, the woodland caribou, have gone. Once they moved through the forests in a living wave of flesh, and their twice yearly migrations in search of food spelled life itself to the natives along their routes. The coming of the deer was an eagerly awaited event, and although each year the Indians took their toll of beasts, they made no inroads on their numbers.

It may have been the change in the environment that caused the woodland caribou to disappear, but there is another, grimmer chapter in the saga of the caribou for which there is less excuse. It was with firearms supplied by the white man that the Chippewa were able to drive the Sioux west from the Great Lakes, and not unnaturally, the Chippewa used these firearms to kill game as well as their fellow-men. The invention and sale of the repeating rifle to the Indian meant that he was able to kill more game, faster. Even then, all might have been well, for the Indian would not have bothered to kill more game than he could eat.

To encourage the sale of ammunition, the trading posts that were springing up all over the territory offered to buy back all the caribou tongues the Indians could bring in. So every winter the hunters set out, each armed with a .30–30 rifle and a thousand rounds of ammunition. They waited for the coming of the deer, and where the caribou crossed a stream or were crammed into a narrow defile, they slaughtered them until the streams were blocked and the corpses beyond counting.

All this happened just fifty years ago. In view of the record, there is grim humor in the Boundary Waters Canoe Area Plan Environmental Statement. In listing the species of fauna in need of preservation, it allots the caribou six words:

Woodland caribou. Not present. Complete protection.

This, briefly, was one chapter in the complex history of the North woods through which I now journeyed. I was lost somewhere in a scattering of islands that lay spread across the lake, a profusion of tumbled stone and dense forests linked by a tortuous network of channels and inlets so interwoven that it was impossible to see where the islands ended and the mainland began. Behind me lay days of travel, of long journeys across lakes and down rivers, over portage trails rutted and mired with the tracks of moose. Time had dissolved into a changing kaleidoscope of misty dawns—chill with the bite of early frosts—long days of sunshine and a clean cold wind, nights filled with firelight and the white blaze of the stars. Scenes of woodland and lakeland, of barren rock and foaming water, of placid, winding rivers spattered with the emerald leaves of lilies—all had blended and merged into one.

The sun was setting, and around me, my camp was secure, the tent pitched, gear stowed away, and the canoe beached—turned upside down and looking like a great silver sturgeon stranded on the shore. The embers of the cooking fire glowed red among the stones, and a yellow tongue of flame licked out and devoured a stray piece of birch bark that lay among the ashes.

The lake lay still, a dark mirror to the trees. The island was bathed in golden light, and the trunks of the pines glowed richly red. Tall grasses, tawny as a lion's mane, their tips ruby-tinged, stood sentinel beside the bleached, bare rocks.

A kingfisher plummeted into the lake, falling from the sky in a long, slanting, spiraling dive that ended in a fountain of silver spray, and the reflection of the trees danced attendance on the widening ripples that spread away into the shadows of the approaching night. Somewhere a loon called a mocking challenge to the skies, and a jay answered in a thin, dry voice that was lost in the emptiness of space.

This was the wilderness experience, and it was to be mine only for a brief space of time, for afterward, no record, no image preserved on film, no written description, no feat of memory could recall the experience in full. Visions would linger, tantalizingly inadequate, a sound or scent would stir awakening memories, but after a brief moment, recollection would fail.

Some wilderness must remain, and not just for the sake of man alone. Places where man must go, if he goes at all, with humility, and reverence, and respect. Places in this world which are not his, but which he guards to ensure the safety of the rest of the living world and which he may enter only as an honored and privileged guest. For either a wilderness is a wilderness, or it isn't, and if it isn't, then there is no reason to go in search of its special qualities.

Multipurpose use of land may win votes, but it tears the living heart out of the wild. Build highways, holiday homes, and campsites, and the tourists will come, but they will not experience the wilderness, for the wilderness will have already been destroyed.

Even here, in the vast roadless expanse of the forest, the land bore the scars of man's passing. Campsites were worn bare, portages rutted and eroded, landings churned into a sour waste of mud. The forest was too accessible, and technological improvements, lightweight gear, dehydrated foods, and efficient clothing made wilderness travel perhaps too easy. Even with the restrictions already in force, pressures on the environment were bound to grow as more and more people came from the towns and cities.

Already there were signs that certain sections of the forest would benefit from being closed to mankind for an indefinite period, yet to do this would increase the pressures on those areas remaining open. The strain, it seems, can only be relieved by designating more wilderness areas, or by limiting the numbers of those desiring entry at any one time.

If the human population of the world were evenly distributed over the available land surface, each individual would have about six acres, not to call his own, but to share with the rest of the living world. Fortunately for mankind and the environment, man prefers to crowd together, to assemble in close-knit communities. Yet we would do well to remember that we have, perhaps, witnessed the last great emigrations of man. For the first time in the history of the world, there is no place left to go, no new continents to discover. We must make the most of what we have.

Meanwhile, although regrettably, certain areas, because of past mistakes or mismanagement, must be closed to mankind, I would not bar man from the wilderness entirely, for it cannot be denied that as an indigenous species of this planet, he has an inalienable right to go there. To go, but not to exploit or to harm. To take nothing. To absorb the spirit of the wild.

12

The Harvest of Fur

It had been raining since dawn, and the woodlands were without shadow—the light softened and diffused so that even the scarlet splendor of the bunchberries lacked its usual hard brilliance. The gray of the river reflected the overcast skies, and the reedy margins of the beaver ponds were white against the dark mantle of the pines.

I emerged from a portage to find the river flowing at right angles to the trail. It had shrunk considerably in size; the current was barely perceptible, and the waters were so shallow as to be scarcely deep enough to float the canoe. The map I carried had long since ceased to agree with the terrain I was crossing, and for many hours and even more miles, I had been unsure of my whereabouts. Now I hesitated, uncertain whether this was the main river or an unmarked tributary. What current there was seemed to flow in the right direction so I decided to press on, even though it meant having to wade through the icy water, dragging my canoe behind me until the water grew deep enough to allow me to paddle again.

As it happened, I had chosen the right route and came at

last to a lake I could identify on the map. Fortunately for my peace of mind, I was unaware at the time that there exists in the North woods a river which the Indians used to call the Echimamish, the river that flows both ways. This river was made navigable solely by the efforts of the beaver, who had so dammed the stream that canoeists, ascending one dam after another, suddenly came upon one dam facing the other way, and the current flowing in the opposite direction.

The weary traveler, finding his way upstream barred by a tangled mass of logs and branches over which he has to haul his canoe and gear, might often curse the industry of these out-size rodents, but without them, especially in the late summer, he would find the way impassable, with only a trickle of water above the bare bedrock. Sometimes this happens—where a trapper has illegally dynamited the dam to get at the beaver—and then the only recourse is to portage, either along the bed of the river or by hacking a trail through the woods.

So the beaver is a good friend to the canoeist, as he was to the Indian. In fact, it may be true to say that the beaver was responsible for the invention of the canoe, for no other form of transport would be of the slightest use, in summertime at any rate, over that region of water, swamp, and narrow, winding woodland trails.

The canoe is efficient, and it is easily constructed by a capable craftsman equipped only with primitive, Stone Age tools. All the materials are readily available—birch bark for the skin, cedar for the framework, pitch pine for sealing, and wattape, the fibrous roots of the spruce, for stitching the bark to the ribbing. Though fragile, it is easy to repair, and if the damage is too great, the canoe can be written off without being considered too great a loss. Before the throwaway container and the ball point pen, man had invented the disposable boat, with this difference: No fossil fuels had been used in its manufacture, and the materials were impeccably biodegradable.

With the aid of their canoes, the Indians journeyed through the North woods, fishing, hunting, and harvesting the wild rice that grew by the lake edge. They trapped the beaver, not only for their flesh, but for the pelts, which, while not so luxuriant as those of other fur-bearing animals, were supple and warm, making ideal robes and bedcoverings. When, after a few seasons' use, the pelts became shabby and worn and all the guard hairs on the fur had been rubbed away, the Indians discarded them and made new robes.

Meanwhile, the white man had begun to realize the immensity and the wealth of the fur harvest to be reaped from the North American continent, and in 1670 King Charles II of England granted a Royal Charter to "The Governer and Company of Adventurers of England Trading into Hudson's Bay." This later became known as "The Hudson's Bay Company," or more simply the H.B.C.

For years the company operated under conditions of intense rivalry with other organizations, most notably the Northwesters, founded in 1874 under the leadership of one Ben Pond, and the XY Company, headed by Alexander Mackenzie. Eventually these two companies united to form the Northwest Company, which in turn merged with The Hudson's Bay Company in 1821.

For centuries, Europe had been starved of fur, as populations grew and the indigenous fur-bearing mammals were trapped out. All skins were in demand—fox and fisher, marten and ermine and mink, lynx and muskrat, otter, wolf, and bear—but the pelts most wanted, the ones most plentiful and easy to obtain, in fact, the very bread and butter of the fur trade, were those of the beaver.

The value of the beaver pelt lay in the underfur. Each hair was finely barbed, making the pelt into a dense, tightly woven wooly mat, and it was this underfur that was considered uniquely suitable for the making of felt. This was then pressed and molded into thick, firm felt hats to grace the heads of rich and fashionable men and women all over Europe. So began a slaughter that was to continue for over two hundred years, a massacre motivated solely by vanity and greed. No amount of romanticism about the voyageurs of the fur trade era, no admiration for the courage of the northern trappers, no respect for the business acumen that organized the trade can quite overcome the distaste I feel whenever I look back over this era. I feel neither guilt nor remorse, only regret that the white man found the practice to be necessary, and worse, that he had to implicate the Indian in his crimes.

The trading began innocently enough and can best be imagined, perhaps, through the eyes of an old North woods Indian as he sits outside his tepee on a fine morning in early summer, just after the breakup of the ice. His shoulders are protected from the lingering chill of a late frost by his old beaver robe, and he fingers the fur fondly, noting regretfully that the guard hairs are all gone and that he must provide himself with a new robe before autumn.

His gentle reverie is disturbed by the outbreak of a commotion on the shores of the lake and the appearance in the camp of two white men, the first he has ever seen. His interest in their appearance, in their bearded faces and ragged garments, is soon replaced by a more critical consideration of their implements and weapons. A practical man, he has only to cut himself once on a steel-bladed knife to realize that this is an infinitely superior tool to his own stone knife, while the small iron cooking pots carried by the white men are to him a singularly startling invention. Hitherto, he and his tribe had heated water and cooked food in logs hollowed out and heated with hot stones. These pots could be carried by the braves on a hunting expedition or war party, and used again and again. What could the white man want in trade for goods of such value? His tepee? His canoe? His daughter?

Imagine the astonishment of the old man when he discovered that in return for such wealth the white man wanted, not something of any value at all, but the old beaver robe he had that very morning decided he must throw away! If there did not exist already an Indian adage similar to the old saying that a fool and his money are soon parted, one would have been born at that moment!

So a brisk trade began and, as it developed, so the value in trade of the beaver skin became established. Worn robes, comprising six to eight skins, still fetched the highest price, for what the Indians did not know was that in the felt industry the guard hairs were a nuisance and costly to remove, and old robes, from which the guard hairs had worn or slipped, were more easily processed. Soon however, Indians were trapping beaver and exchanging the dried pelts in trade.

For twenty good skins, a brave could get himself a musket; one skin would buy him ten musket balls and another half-pint of powder. Three skins would buy him a good steel ax head, while ten would buy him a woolen blanket to replace the beaver robe he had parted with. It is interesting to note that whereas once the Indian took eight skins with which to clothe himself, he now needed ten to obtain an inferior garment. Thus do the economics of capitalism work against the environment.

The fur trade grew, and so began the era of the voyageur, for though the English were content to sit in their trading posts and wait for the Indians to come to them, the traders of the Northwest Company went out to meet the Indians. Each spring, as soon as the ice broke, the voyageurs set off in giant thirty-six-foot canoes, carrying a cargo of three tons of trade goods.

Before them lay a journey of a thousand miles—from Montreal along the river Ottawa, up the Mattawa River to Trout Lake, then by portage to Lake Nipissing. From there they paddled down French River to Lake Huron, and through the North Channel to Saulte Ste. Marie. There they portaged around the rapids, and finally, paddled four hundred and fifty miles across Lake Superior to Grand Portage.

Each canoe carried a crew of eight to ten men—French Canadians—who shared the task of paddling and portaging the canoe and its cargo. They were, in the main, short, stocky men of immense stamina and toughness. The cargo was divided into ninety-pound bales, and each man carried at least two of these bales on portage, hung by a tumpline from his forehead. Often, to save time, a man would carry more. The record appears to be held by one George Bonga, who, for a wager, carried nine bales, eight hundred and ten pounds, for a mile uphill.

If these men were hard, the men they met at Grand Portage in mid-July were even tougher. These men of the north brought the furs out of the North woods, packed in the standard ninety-pound bales, and transported in smaller, twenty-five-foot canoes, manned by a crew of five or six men. Some had traveled the entire two thousand miles from Lake Athabasca, and were anxious to exchange their furs for trade goods and begin the return journey with all speed. There was always the fear that the early onset of winter would encase them in its icy tomb. This could mean starvation and death, at very least, the humiliation and degradation of having to eat crow—often the only food obtainable in the frozen forest. Small wonder that the men of the north regarded their compatriots from Montreal with some contempt, referring to them as "eaters of pork," who spent their winters living soft.

On the whole, the voyageurs got on well with the Indians, often taking native women as wives and treating the men as brothers. Indeed, it was the Indian who taught the voyageur his trade, taught him to make his canoe and guided him through the maze of waterways and portages that linked the lakes. Without the active cooperation of the Indian, there could not have been such a rich traffic in furs.

At the height of the fur trade, some two hundred thousand beaver skins—in addition to other furs—were being shipped from the continent each year. Each beaver pelt was worth anything from four to ten dollars.

The year 1820 saw the invention of the silk hat, which replaced the beaver hat in high society. Although the fur trade was to flourish for another fifty years, it had passed its peak, and by the end of the century, the era of the voyageur had gone.

So, too, had the beavers, along with a host of other fur-bearing animals. The lodges of the beavers, empty now, fell into grassy ruin, and their dams crumbled and rotted away. The creeks dwindled and dried, and the beaver ponds became meadows of scrub and coarse grass. In many areas, game which had been dependent on the beaver for their water supplies now moved away, and in the empty, arid woodlands, the risk of fire increased.

Today, thanks to rigorous conservation measures, the beaver is returning to the North woods, and as I journeyed along the waterways nearly a century after the last songs of the voyageurs had echoed across the lakes, I saw beaver signs in plenty. I crossed beaver dams and passed their lodges. I disturbed young beavers feeding on water plants, and at night, as I lay in my sleeping bag, I heard the slap of their tails on the water of the lake.

Yet I could not rid myself of the feeling that, on the whole, life in the woodlands was less plentiful than it might be, than it was before the coming of the fur traders. Each morning, I was up before dawn. Each night, I lay in wait, watching and listening until it grew too dark to see. I watched an osprey hunting for food, its dives more spectacular than successful. A dozen times it soared into the sky, circled around, and plunged down into the lake before flapping off, fishless, over the trees.

I saw mink and grouse, chipmunks, squirrels, and a salamander. After the rain, small, varicolored frogs emerged, and at night, by the light of a torch, I watched crayfish feeding in the shallow waters of the lake. Occasionally, I disturbed a garter snake.

Birds I found in plenty—blue jays and gray jays, woodpeckers and sapsuckers, heron, kingfisher, merganser, and loon. Of larger game, I saw nothing, no evidence of deer, although signs of moose were plentiful. From time to time, I came upon the droppings of wolves and the unmistakable prints of their pads. They were around, although they did not betray their presence by sight or sound. Once I knew that I was in close proximity to a mother bear and her cub, so close that a little puddle of urine passed by the infant had not yet begun to soak into the soil. I stayed very still and waited with mixed feelings of anxiety and hope, but nothing stirred among the trees.

Perhaps the game was there all the time and merely hidden from my eyes. Yet it was as if I had arrived in the North woods soon after the passing of a new Ice Age, when the glaciers of greed and commerce had ground over the land. Slowly, the forests were being repopulated, but the task was not yet complete.

Or perhaps it was. Perhaps the intricate pattern of the environment was now rewoven, but in a changed, simpler design. Certainly the Chippewa would never again follow the hunting trails of his ancestors or sit outside his tepee wearing his beaver skin robe. Or would he? Who knows what changes another ten thousand years may see.

That night, I camped beneath a stand of virgin pine. Their massive trunks, wider than I could span with my outstretched arms, towered to the sky. Beneath them, the ground was bare save for a soft carpet of needles. The air was sweet with an incenselike perfume, and there was no sound save for the hushed sigh of the wind, the whispers of gods of earth and sky, secrets of the immortal.

If I were to fell these trees and make a fire of the trunks and branches, I would commit no great crime against the environment, for in the brief space of a few hundred years, a new generation of pines would grow to full maturity and all would be the same. My crime would be against my fellow-men, for once the pines were destroyed, no man alive today could live long enough to see them replaced. I would have destroyed more than the pines. I would have taken away the chance for my fellow-men to share the numinous beauty and grandeur of these trees.

Our lives are too short and fleeting for us to enjoy the luxury of witnessing the processes of slow change. If I could look forward to a life expectancy of ten thousand years, events which now seem catastrophic might well be minimized. On the other hand, the long-term consequences of man's actions could well assume greater importance. Since, in a sense, we all live on in our sons and daughters, we should perhaps begin to cultivate the outlook of one who expects to survive for ninety centuries or more.

13

The Poison on the Plains

The pelt of the beaver was not the only fur to excite the avarice of the white man, nor was the harvest confined to the North woods. To the south lay the Great Plains of the Midwest, a vast, empty, rolling expanse of prairie, the land of the buffalo. For untold centuries, they peopled the plains, the canyons thundered to the sound of their passing, and the dust clouds raised by the trampling of their hooves hung on the horizon long after they had gone. Always, the wolf packs kept company with the herds.

Apart from its own kin, the wolf was probably the first animal a buffalo calf ever saw. Each day throughout its life, the wolves would be there, familiar but respectful, waiting for the first sign of weakness, the first hint of infirmity or disease. Then for the buffalo, its last sight on earth would be the wolf pack, closing in.

The buffalo herd was its own protection. At the moment of its birth, the calf would be surrounded by adults of the tribe, moving around in a close-knit circle, protecting the youngster from attack. The same adults would stay with the calf until it was strong enough to join the main herd. Only when it was too old or too weak from injury or disease would the herd desert one of its kind, and then the wolves would bring swift release from pain.

Each event, birth and death, was recorded on the prairie. During the waiting time of birth, the droppings of the buffalo and the trampling of their hooves spread a circle of fertility over the waiting ground. Likewise, in death, the scattered remains—the calcium, and the phosphates, and nitrates, the elements which once were living flesh—soaked into the ground along with shreds of hair matted with seeds and burrs. So each drama was commemorated annually by a rebirth of life, and the circle knew no end.

Like the wolves, small bands of red men also followed the buffalo, killing them with primitive weapons or stampeding a herd over a cliff. Buffalo meat provided their food, the hides their tepees and clothes. They used the sinews for sewing thread and wove wool from the hair. The dung they used as fuel and the bladders as drinking vessels. The Indians have been described as poor and wretched, and poor they certainly were, by material standards. Whether they were wretched is a matter of opinion.

Then the Spaniards reached America, and they brought with them the horse. Some horses the Indians acquired by barter, some they stole. Others escaped and bred wild, and from these "mestenos," or mustangs, the Indians built up their herds. After the Spaniards came settlers, pushing west with their wagon trains, and soon, in addition to horses, the Indians obtained firearms.

For a brief while, the Plains Indian enjoyed an era of affluence unknown in the history of America. Their story, the short but bloody drama enacted between them, the white man, and the buffalo, is now well known, ending in the extermination of the Indian, the buffalo, and the long grass prairie. The fate of the wolf is less often recounted.

The Indians themselves killed wolves for their warm, luxurious fur, and the white man was at pains to exterminate every one he came across, if only to safeguard his livestock.

Then, in 1847, a ship with a strange cargo sailed from Philadelphia en route for South America. News that gold had been discovered in California reached the vessel, and it diverted to San Francisco. So the first shipment of strychnine reached the Far West.

The use of the drug as a poison had long been known in the Old World, and doubtless it had been widely used in the early days of the Colonies. Certainly, the demand for strychnine was high enough for the firm of Rosengarten and Denis to start manufacturing it in Philadelphia in 1834. It was to prove so effective in killing animals that, by 1860, its use had spread from the Atlantic to the Pacific, and from Texas in the south to the Arctic regions.

Strychnine sulphate is a white, crystalline powder with an intensely bitter taste. It is derived from a tropical tree, the *strychnos nux vomica,* which grows up to forty-five feet in height, and is found in India, North Australia, and Cochin China. The fruit resembles an orange and contains numerous disklike seeds of a grayish-brown color. It is from these seeds—variously known as Quaker or bachelor buttons, dog button, vomit nut or vomiting bean—that the poison is derived.

To join the colorful, lawless throng that slowly spread west across the prairie came the professional wolfer. Equipped with a horse, a rifle, a supply of stores, and a plentiful supply of strychnine, he followed the buffalo herds, shooting a few individual ones, ripping open the carcasses, and lacing them liberally with the poison. The following morning, the wolfer would visit each carcass in turn, collect the bodies of the wolves, and skin them.

In winter, the wolfers lived in semidugouts which offered them some shelter from the bitter cold and the fierce blizzards that raged across the prairie, and which hid them from the keen eyes of wandering Indians. Here, too, they could bring the bodies of the wolves to thaw out before skinning.

It was a rough, hard life, but the rewards were considerable. Up to sixty wolves might be poisoned in one night, and the value of one winter's haul of pelts was in the region of four thousand dollars. One night's harvest in Kansas realized eighty-two wolf pelts worth two dollars and fifty cents apiece. As a bonus, the wolfers harvested many smaller pelts—coyote, kit fox, gray and red fox; the bodies of eagles, hawks, magpies, and ravens which had also died while feeding on the poisoned meat were left to rot or to poison other carrion feeders in their turn.

At the end of the American Civil War, the ranks of the wolfers were swelled by ex-soldiers, ex-beaver trappers from the north, outlaws, and ne'er-do-wells. Slowly, they moved north from Texas to Kansas, through Montana up to Manitoba, and on the way, they earned the antipathy of the Plains Indian. The red men saw their herds dwindle as the wolfers shot buffalo for bait. Their ponies sickened and died from cropping grass where the poison lingered for weeks or even months, sun-dried, but still active.

The old, amiable relations between the white and the red man had turned sour. Very early in his acquaintance with the settlers, the Indian had discovered the delights of strong drink for the French carried brandy and the English rum to sustain them on their rigorous journeys. The drinking probably started innocently enough, with wandering bands of Indians sharing a convivial evening with the members of a wagon train. Sometimes, however, it happened that supplies of drink were short, or the leader of a band, knowing the effects of strong drink on his men, deliberately asked the settlers to water it down. Inevitably, misunderstandings arose, and fights broke out.

Then the whiskey traders moved in, bartering their firewater for buffalo hides and tongues. An Indian with a pony and a gun could assure himself of a steady supply of drink, but one whose pony had been poisoned or who had bartered away all his possessions soon found his supplies cut off. So the Indians stole the horses of the wolfers, and the wolfers exacted revenge on both Indian and whiskey trader alike. In an attempt to restore order and curtail the activities of the whiskey traders, the Northwest Mounted Police were formed in 1872, later becoming the Royal Canadian Mounted Police.

The wolfers themselves were not immune to the wares of the whiskey traders. A recipe for Indian whiskey still exists, and it is worth recording, if not reproducing:

> To one barrel of Missouri river water add two gallons of alcohol, two ounces of strychnine, three plugs of tobacco, and five bars of soap to give it a bread. Then stir in half a pound of red pepper. Add sagebrush, boil until the mixture turns brown, strain, and bottle.

Strychnine was used as a stimulant and the tobacco to produce nausea, for Indians at that time believed no whiskey to be of value unless it made you deathly sick. It was said of the white man that, when he drank it, he became so inebriated that he could not close his eyes. The price for a bottle was one buffalo robe, but naturally as the buyer grew drunker, the price went up. This particular concoction was never sold anywhere except from trading posts along the Missouri River, but doubtless other brews were just as lethal.

The era of the wolfer, the buffalo, and the Plains Indian passed, and in their place came vast herds of domestic cattle, as the rancher and the cowboy took over the prairie. The wolf packs that remained turned their attention to this new and easily available supply of beef; so, it became an unwritten law of the range that no cowboy would pass the carcass of a steer without stopping and lacing the body with a liberal dose of strychnine in the hope of eliminating yet one more wolf.

No account was taken of the loss of other wildlife by this practice, or of the manner of their dying, although it was impossible to insure that each victim assimilated an immediately fatal dose. In minute quantities, taken over a period of time, strychnine sharpens mental powers and increases sensibility so that sight and hearing are improved, and the sense of touch becomes more acute. The heart beats more quickly and strongly, the breathing becomes deeper, and bowel movements less sluggish. Reflex actions are increased, the muscles develop greater tone, and there is a general sense of increased bodily well being.

Larger, toxic doses lead to nightmare as the drug acts on the central nervous system, lowering the normal threshold for impulse transmission and causing increased excitability of all reflex mechanisms. The poisoned animal salivates, vomits, and strains to evacuate its bowels. The slightest stimulation—a faint noise, a gentle breeze—sets the heart racing and the lungs gasping for air, while the muscles knot into cramping convulsion, crippling, choking, causing acute pain. The victim is conscious to the end.

Yet it may be that such an end was more merciful than some of those devised by man for the wolf. In addition to traps, snares, pitfalls, and deadfalls as well as lassoing, shooting, and hunting the wolf with hounds, man was ever seeking to find new ways to rid himself of the wolf; nowhere was his ingenuity ever tempered by mercy. A favorite method was to conceal several large fishhooks in a ball of fat and to suspend the bait by a strong line from a branch. Any wolf leaping up and snapping the bait hung there until he died.

Sharp knife blades were planted in the frozen ground and

the cutting edge buried in frozen meat. A wolf licking the frozen bait lacerated its tongue until it bled to death. Yet another practice was to coil a length of whalebone into a spring, tie it with gut, and bury it in a ball of fat. The wolf ate the bait and, when its digestive juices dissolved the gut, the whalebone sprang out straight.

The early explorers soon discovered that the wolf would readily mate with the domestic dog. The resulting offspring, although of nervous disposition, were strong and hardy workers. It was not unusual to leave a bitch in heat tied up outside the cabin in the hope that it would attract the attention of a he-wolf. A variation of this practice was to wait until the couple were actually tied, and then to rush out and club the wolf to death.

One final account serves to indicate that man's antipathy to the wolf is not yet dead. "A party of deer hunters coming upon a she wolf giving birth to cubs, one member drew his hunting knife and slit the wolf's throat, then stamped on the surviving pups." This is not an anecdote handed down from the distant past. It happened in Minnesota in 1973. Although most deer hunters would disassociate themselves from such behavior, and indeed, wonder what deerhunters were doing in the woods at a time when wolf cubs were being born, the fact remains. The North woods cover a large area and the conservation officers cannot be everywhere at once.

Slowly but surely, the wolf has been exterminated from state after state. At one time, the value of the pelt was sufficient to attract the attentions of the wolfers, and for a while, the fur trade was brisk. The United States even supplied wolf furs to the Russian Army.

As the value of the pelt declined and wolves became scarcer and harder to catch, so the wolfers turned to other ways of making a living. To maintain the pressure on the wolf, various bounty schemes were introduced, both by individual states and by cattlemen's associations. Even today, the cattlemen form perhaps the strongest lobby against any legislation to protect the wolf.

The late Aldo Leopold, writing about the grizzly bear, said, "There seems to be a tacit assumption that if Grizzlies survive in Canada and Alaska, that is good enough. It is not good enough for me. . . . Relegating grizzlies to Alaska is like relegating happiness to heaven; one may never get there." (*A Sand County Almanac.*)

Leopold's comment on relegating grizzlies to Alaska applies equally to wolves relegated to Minnesota, to which I would add, "Even if you get there, you may not find them."

14

Wild Fire

Now there was no moon, and above the clearing, the tops of the pines were lost in a dark void in which millions of stars burned with a white glory such as I had never seen before. The rock at my back was cold; the red glow of the fire was just one more star in the limitless ocean of space.

I was marooned on an island of warmth and light, and, although tired, I was curiously reluctant to let the fire die down. I knew that it would take a conscious effort of will to abandon the flames, even for the greater comfort and warmth of my sleeping bag.

I threw another log onto the blaze and watched as thousands of hours of stored sunlight—energy accumulated from out of space—were released in an explosion of heat and light. The log was mostly cellulose, carbon, hydrogen, and oxygen. Although sun-dried, it contained moisture which would evaporate in the heat, and more water would be formed as the hydrogen released by the fire combined with the oxygen in the air around the flames.

The cellulose molecule is long, and immensely complicated, with thousands of atoms strung together like a rope of pearls. When heated, the molecules on the surface become agitated—whirling, vibrating, twisting, and writhing—until they begin to snap. Tens of millions of carbon particles, incandescent with heat, flame into light and waver above the log, as all around them hundreds of chemical reactions take place.

Hydrogen unites with oxygen to form water. Carbon joins with hydrogen to form a number of compounds, among them methane, ethane, propane, butane, pentane, hexane, heptane, and octane. Gasoline, in fact, is being formed in the heat of the blaze and instantly converted to carbon dioxide and water.

To stare into the flames is to witness again the dawn of creation, to see the world shrouded by reeking mists and clouds of vapor, a world of moist, steamy heat, redolent with the smell of sulphur and marsh gas, a rich bubbling broth of chemical activity in which the giant carbon molecules formed and reformed, grouped and broke away until, at last, life took form. It must have been a world of little light, as the dense clouds of vapor created by burning gases blotted out the sun. It was a world without oxygen, for this gas had been consumed in the fires of creation. These first beginnings of life must have been anaerobic, and to them, the oxygen synthesized by the chlorophyll-producing plants which had begun to evolve must have been as dangerous and toxic as carbon dioxide or sulphur dioxide is to us. It was the first faint flush of green that spread over the oceans in response to the pale light of the sun emerging from the primeval mists that ordained the future of men and wolves.

The flames flicker and fade, the metals in the wood lend color to the wavering tongues of light—yellow for sodium, green for copper, blue and violet for potassium. The unburned carbon has vanished as smoke, and all that remains is a handful of gray ash, less than one per cent of the original log, a rich blend of minerals, potassium, phosphorous, sulphur, copper, silicon, magnesium, boron, and sodium, the basic ingredients for a new forest.

In burning, the log has produced more than twice its own weight in material, most of it water and carbon dioxide, which, if it could be collected and poured back on the blaze, would be more than sufficient to extinguish it. So the first fires of creation must have died.

Until a couple of centuries ago, wood was the main source of energy in the world. There are those who maintain that it could still be so; that a thirtieth of the annual growth of all the trees in the world could produce enough alcohol to run every industry, every airplane, and every automobile that now uses coal or petroleum.

Yet the fascination of fire for man goes beyond recognition of its utility, beyond scientific interest to a world beyond reason, a world where fire was sacred, to be worshiped rather than harnessed as an energy source. The relationship between fire and man, especially in the early days, gives rise to endless speculation, for without it, man could not have hoped to begin his climb toward civilization.

Fire has run wild over the earth since the time of creation, set free by spontaneous combustion or lightning strike. Primitive man must have noticed that a bush fire would drive before it a panic-stricken population of animals, many of which could easily be caught. He must have noticed, too, like the crows and the ravens, that in the smoking embers left behind after the fire had passed were the charred corpses of lizards and birds, rodents and insects, that had perished in the flames. These were edible, and maybe man relished the piquant taste. From here, it was but a short step to collecting and hoarding fire, then deliberately starting grass and bush fires as part of the hunting program.

Perhaps man's habit of cooking his meat started in this manner, or perhaps other forces were at work. As a hunter, man enjoyed his meat hot and bloody. Stale meat, several days old, cold and rubbery, the blood and fat congealed among the muscle fibers was possibly less acceptable to his palate. Maybe, in the beginning, man did not cook his meat so much as reheat it.

I find it hard to believe that man adopted fire as a means of protection. Predatory animals do not fear fire as such; they fear the presence of man, and fire betrays that presence. What is more, smoke during the day and firelight at night, by revealing the whereabouts of man to his human enemies, have caused more deaths than ever occurred from attack by wild animals. Yet man persisted in hugging his fire, and, in doing so, isolated himself from the night. Fire bred fear and a dread of the dark shadows that lay beyond the circle of light, where every rock and shrub was a lurking beast and every rustle the threat of an impending foe. Other species welcome the darkness as a protective cloak. They do not fear the shadows. They know that it is in the moonlight and the open spaces that bright death waits.

To survive as a species, man had no need of fire. Proof of this lies in the life style of the Eskimo, who, of all races on this earth, stood to benefit most from the warmth and comfort of fire. In the winter, the Eskimo could not have fire, for there was nothing to burn at the time when it would appear that he needed it most. So although he knew the art of making fire, the Eskimo came to rely instead on the insulating properties of snow, of the cunning use of fur garments, and the bodily heat generated by a diet rich in oils, fats, and meat protein.

Other primitive communities never learned the art of making fire, and even today carry a supply in the form of a torch or a bowl of glowing embers. There are also whole nations who have lost the art, who rely entirely on the manufacture of matches and cigarette lighters. It is not uncommon today to find small urban enclaves of nonsmokers who have no means whatever in their immediate possession to make fire. They have no need for it. The wheel of evolution has gone full circle.

All the same, fire worship dies hard in man. Little boys will always play with matches, and adults who have been raised amid urban central heating, who scarcely ever set eyes on a naked flame, will, at the first opportunity, light a fire of small sticks and sit around while the smoke smarts their eyes, poking fresh twigs into the blaze.

Fire has been part of the natural cycle in the North woods since the passing of the Ice Age. It is part of the environmental process, yet another factor that assists the program of early obsolescence. To the logger, a stand of giant white pine is a profitable investment. To the poet, it is a source of beauty and inspiration. To the environment, it is an anachronism, a monoculture serving only its own ends. Precious nutrients lie locked in the trees, minerals that should be circling faster through the biosphere. The dense crowns of the pines shut out the light of the sun, and the forest floor is shaded and dim, too dark for photosynthesis to take place, for flowers and grasses and ferns to grow.

The environment has many ways of correcting such a situation. Disease may attack the crowns of the trees. A tornado may cut its highway of devastation through the stand. Qali, the dense, sticky snow that falls in calm weather, may cling to the branches of a tree, and by its own weight bring the tree down. Fire is perhaps the greatest controlling force of all, and contrary to popular belief, lightning does strike the same place twice; over the millennia, many, many times.

Left to itself, the forest might, on average, be wholly burned over once every hundred years. The important words to remember in this context are "on average," for while one area might be burned three times in a century, another might survive untouched for three hundred years. Foresters, who even now are studying the effects of controlled burning in the North woods and contemplating its use in silviculture, are conscious that it is not easy to emulate the forces of the environment.

To witness a forest fire is perhaps one of the most awesome experiences known to man. There must be few indeed who can remain sufficiently detached from the destruction and the devastation, the suffering of all forms of life, to foresee any advantage emerging from the inferno. Afterward, as the stark skeletons of the trees stand scarred above a dark wilderness where no bird sings, it seems that life has been snuffed out entirely.

Yet this is not so, and, within weeks, the wilderness will have started to spring up again, as the sun warms the soil, and millions of waiting seeds, unharmed by the fire, burgeon into growth. The benison of minerals left in the ash, equivalent to years of accumulation by slow decay, brings on a rapid surge of growth, a feast of vegetation to which the animals of the forest soon return.

The last serious outbreak of fire in the Superior National Forest occurred east of the Little Indian Sioux River. Fanned by winds gusting up to thirty miles an hour, the blaze raged for three days, eventually destroying twenty-five square miles of forest. Scientists are still studying the long-term effects of the blaze, yet they would be the first to admit that no two fires are alike in behavior or consequence.

Over the ages, fire has shaped the basic character of the forest. Some species, such as spruce and fir, are highly vulnerable to the flames, and healthy growth for them depends on the virtual absence of fire. Yet aspen, birch, and jack pine, though vulnerable by themselves, have survived as a species through countless burnings. The roots of aspen and birch remain alive in the soil, even though the tree itself may have been totally destroyed, and the roots send forth suckers so fast that these gain a head start over other species and quickly become dominant after a blaze. Although the jack pine may be destroyed as a tree, its seeds survive; indeed, they need heat to be able to start to germinate, and after a burn, the clearings may be thickly carpeted with jack pine seedlings, sometimes as many as twenty thousand to an acre.

Individual red and white pines may well survive a blaze, for both species have thick, insulating bark which protects the vital inner ring of cambium from excess heat. Moreover, once they have reached a certain height, their crowns are sufficiently remote from the tinder of the forest floor to survive any ordeal save that of a crown fire. So today, giants survive, their trunks scarred with the rings of ancient fires.

Fire releases nutrients, recycles energy in the biosphere; yet, it is important to remember that fire puts nothing back into the environment that was not already there. In fact, following a fire, there is always a small loss of nutrients, a runoff of minerals dissolved in rainwater and carried by the rivers to the sea. On level ground, this is slight. In mountain areas, it can be disastrous, and many places in the world have been condemned to environmental and social poverty as a result of deforestation and erosion.

There is no doubt that the Indian deliberately started forest fires to encourage new growth to attract game, create clearings for the growing of maize, perhaps to make for themselves a habitat in which it was less easy for an enemy to approach. There is plentiful evidence to suggest that man, particularly primitive man, feared the forests and the trees. The Indians of the north believed that no man could survive more than five days in the forests. If the dreaded Wendigo did not claim him, he would assuredly go mad. Gypsies in England still maintain that to live too long in the New Forest will lead to disease and death, and there are records reaching back to the Bronze Age of deliberate deforestation campaigns, leading inevitably to a deterioration of the environment. It may be that man, like the beaver and the moose, is driven by a blind biological urge toward obsolescence.

Fortunately for mankind, the Indians were too few and the North woods too vast for them to make much impression on the forests. Fortunately, too, it seems that man is at last learning wisdom, is less eager to alter the pattern of the landscape. For he has learned that the forests form an insulating blanket for the earth as efficient and cozy as the down and feathers on a goose or the Eskimo's parka and mukluks.

15

An Old Madness

Through the mist and the rain, the gray river seemed to stretch interminably away to the south, but in reality, I knew that civilization lay only a few miles distant. My wilderness experience was over for the time, and I was reentering the world of men. My return was tinged with regret, partly because I had failed so far to find a wolf pack, but mainly because I had found a new tranquility, a harmony of mind and body and habitat that I was reluctant to abandon.

I reached the last lake. A canoe lay idle in a backwater, and in the stern was seated a red-jacketed figure, his hands clutching a rifle. Pinned to his back was a white, numbered card—his hunting license. The annual moose hunt had begun.

Moose had been increasing over recent years, and now a limited number of licenses were being issued by lottery, each costing a hundred dollars, each shared by four men, and allowing them to take one moose. Once a moose was shot, it had to be disemboweled, then transported from the wilderness in one piece to be checked for disease and parasites at a clearing station. Only then could the carcass be taken away for butchering and deep-freezing.

It takes but a moment to shoot a moose. Only then does the hard work begin, and if the hunter has dropped his moose in a swamp or in dense brush or, indeed, anywhere his truck cannot go, he may well come to wish he had never set eyes on the animal. The biggest moose I saw lay on a trailer, its massive antlers spread wide, its eyes glazed in death, and its tongue hanging grotesquely from its mouth. This beast had been walking down the road in the early morning, and the hunters had simply stopped their car, got the rifle out of its case, and fired.

My hotel lay close to the clearing station, and later, I was to find myself surrounded by dead moose. The parking lot was full of trucks and trailers—each containing its corpse—and the restaurant was full of hunters. No one looked very happy. Even the waitress had lost her usual sunny disposition. Maybe she didn't like the sight of dead moose or the smell of live hunters. Maybe she was just sick of the slaughter, and, like Henry David Thoreau, believed that all things were better alive than dead, men and moose and pine trees.

The hunters did not seem too happy either. I met one standing morosely on a spit of land by the lake, soaking wet. It was his first time out, and just in case he got himself a moose, he had fitted an outboard motor to the side of his canoe. This would save him the arm-wearying task of paddling back to the landing, towing a heavy carcass behind him.

Unfortunately, in a moment of aberration, he stepped out of the canoe on the same side as the motor. The canoe promptly turned turtle, tipping him into the lake. He then tried to light a fire, but since it had been raining for three days, the best he had managed to achieve was a smoldering mess of damp birch logs, which served no purpose other than that of advertising his presence to every man and beast for miles around. He was looking forward to the end of the day.

Another character I met was complaining bitterly about the quality of the plastic bags issued by the Department of Forestry. His job, apparently, had been to hold the bag open while his companions dropped the warm, wet liver of the moose into it. The liver had gone through the bottom of the bag, slid down his trousers, and come to rest on his smart new hunting boots. His comments, though colorful, must, I fear, go forever unrecorded.

I went along to the clearing station, where a ranger in green overalls and rubber gloves was busy checking hearts and livers for parasites or other evidence of disease. Even with my limited knowledge of pathology, I could tell a diseased liver when I saw one, and most of those I was shown were clearly unfit for consumption.

Nearly all the moose shot had been hit on the trail or on the edges of campsites. They may simply have been unlucky, but it might just be that a heavy infestation of parasites had rendered these individuals just a little less wary, a little less inclined to move away from danger. Was the hunter, like the wolf, culling the less healthy specimens from the stock? The ranger, when I asked him, gave no definite reply, but he agreed that this was the sort of question to which they would like to find the answer.

The modern hunter cannot hope to take the place of the wolf on the ecological carousel. At times in the past, overzealous predator control has led to populations of herbivorous animals reaching pest proportions. Then the hunter feels he is justified in reaching for his rifle. In bookkeeping terms, one error has compensated for the other; yet, the books fail to render a true account.

For the moose is like the pine tree. In life, both serve the environment. The pine shelters the earth, conserves moisture, synthesizes oxygen, and manufactures cellulose from energy derived from the sun. The moose converts cellulose to animal protein via the bacteria in its digestive system, and throughout its life spreads a carpet of fertility over the forest floor. Like the pine tree, the moose, if burned, would, in time, be reduced to a few handfuls of gray ash, but these ashes would be the basic ingredients for a new moose or life in any other of its varied forms.

The wolf kills and gives back to the wild that which belongs to the wild, until his own death cancels out the last of his debts. The hunter kills and takes away that which belongs to the wild. Then via the butcher and the deep freeze, the barbecue and the spit, the transmuted elements of water lily and balsam fir, of blueberry and aspen twig find their way down through the sewers to the sea. A handful of ash, no more, but one vital to the forest, and one that it can ill afford to lose.

When a hunter comes upon the carcass of a deer or moose killed by a wolf pack and left uneaten, he condemns the wolves for killing wastefully. He forgets that, in time, something will eat the corpse—a bear, fox, skunk, a wolverine. In the past, even men have been saved from starvation by coming upon such a kill. The carcass does not belong to man, or wolf, or wolverine but to the living forest of which it is a part.

The modern hunter is caught in a technological trap, and each item of gadgetry acquired—rifle, telescopic sight, camping gear, trailer, pickup, snowmobile, trail bike, canoe, or whatever—detracts rather than adds to the satisfaction of the predatory urge. The man who hunts with a bow and arrow is far closer to his forebears than the man with a carbine. What is more, if the hunter were to cost out the price of his equipment, and account his time and running costs, he would soon find that even at today's prices, it would be cheaper to buy beef.

A hundred years ago, an English writer, a fine naturalist and sportsman, Richard Jefferies, had this to say about the breech-loading shotgun: "The very perfection of our modern guns is to me one of their drawbacks; the use of them is so easy and so certain of effect that it takes away the romance of sport."

Technically, we have come a long way since Richard Jefferies' time. Ethically, we may have taken a step or two back.

The predatory urge dies hard in all of us. Nowhere is it more apparent than in the conservationist, or animal lover, only his quarries are hunters, industry, politicians, and property developers. On the trail, he is indefatigable, and merciless at the kill. He knows the same savage joy in victory as the falcon as it strikes down its prey.

I satisfy my predatory urge by hunting with a camera, and it is my constant companion into the wild, through forests and over mountains, across moorland and along the sea coast. I do not profess to be an expert in its use, but I get a lot of excitement and satisfaction from stalking animals, getting them in my sights, and finally, when the form fills the frame, pressing the shutter release.

I find I enjoy certain advantages over the hunter. I have no closed season or license to worry about, and I can shoot a buck in velvet or a doe with her fawn with as clear a conscience as the hunter when he drops a fully antlered stag. Furthermore, I can fire several times at the same target and so make sure of a really accurate "kill."

Protected species are fair game to me. I can shoot an osprey or a bald eagle, a robin or a cardinal. Species which are worthless to the hunter afford fine sport to the photographer. If anyone doubts my word, he should try shooting chipmunks with a single lens reflex. These rodents seem so readily available, so universally active around the campsite, that they should be easy game. Yet they move so fast, so rarely stay still for more than a moment, that they are extremely difficult to hit. You will waste a lot of film, but providing you do not lose control and hurl your camera at the wretched animal, you can make some good bags.

My collection of trophies occupies no wall space, but fits compactly into a slide box, free from moth and decay. There is no messy butchering involved, no arduous backpacking. A moose weighs exactly the same for me as a butterfly.

A stuffed head is a stuffed head, nothing more. Its surroundings are a wooden plaque and a wall. My trophies, when I project them on a screen, look back at me from the living world to which they belong.

There are snags, many of them shared by the hunter. The light is never quite right for the type of film. The foreground of a picture is often marred by twig or stump which cannot be moved. The range is closer, and the subject is often spooked at the last moment. After a long and arduous stalk, this can be particularly frustrating. The answer, I've found, is to start shooting as soon as the subject is in range, even if the first three exposures show only a tiny dot in the middle of a field of green.

Photography can be more dangerous than hunting with a rifle. You are in closer to the quarry, and while a 150-grain bullet traveling at twenty-six hundred feet per second might stop a charging moose, an exposure of one fiftieth of a second at f/11 most certainly will not! It will make a good picture, but you are unlikely to survive to see it.

All the same, I do not carry a gun, for I believe that to do so is to go halfway to using one. Furthermore, I believe that to go unarmed in search of animals ensures a better chance of success, and barring accidents, guarantees a certain amount of protection. Animals know when a man is dangerous or harmless, and hunting records are full of accounts describing how hunters had searched in vain for their quarry, only to find it, unafraid and unconcerned, at the very moment when their weapons were not to hand.

I do not think there is any mystique about this. To bear arms is second nature to man. Put a man in any situation of danger, and before he seeks a place to hide—before he starts to run—nine times out of ten he will at once look around for a weapon. The moment his hand closes around a club or stick or stone, he feels a little more confident. Even in normal circumstances, it is difficult for a man to resist handling a weapon, be it sword, spear, or repeating rifle. He holds it with a certain respect, even reverence.

A man bearing arms carries himself with an assurance he otherwise lacks. Whether he is conscious of the fact or not, he is at once more dominant, more aggressive, more confident than when he is unarmed. Animals, being the sound judges of character that they are, are quick to sense this aura, and according to their disposition and relative size, stay out of the way or attack.

I sometimes wonder if the animal I'm photographing has "posed" for the camera before. In places like Yellowstone National Park, this must be so, and the quirkiness of human nature is such that when animals are easy to photograph, the hobby loses much of its fascination. No one gets much satisfaction out of shooting a tame bear with a gun or a camera.

I cannot delude myself. When I stalk an animal with a camera, I enjoy the same mixed feelings of exhilaration, fear, and excitement as the man with a gun. I must confess that my equipment costs the same in terms of energy loss, the processing of the films contributes to the pollution of the biosphere, and in truth, I am caught in the same technological trap. My dealer will tell you that I am a hard man to sell gadgets to, but there is one gadget which, if it were available, might help the hunter take the short step toward becoming a photographer, rather than a killer of wildlife. That would be a camera designed as near as possible to resemble a rifle. For the man who wanted to make things really tough for himself, a blank cartridge could be incorporated into the shutter release, so that he only gets one shot. A crazy idea, perhaps, but in this day and age, hunting is a legacy of an old madness, an obsession that drove man out of the warmth and comfort of his cave to hunt the wooly mammoth. Nowadays, it is much cheaper, safer, and more comfortable to shop at the supermarket.

16

The Voice of the Wild

Time was beginning to run out. Soon I would have to leave the North woods and return to my own country. As each day passed, my chances of seeing a wolf seemed to grow more and more remote, but still I persevered in my search, knowing that often, in the past, where intelligence or inspiration has failed, sheer blind obstinacy has brought results.

I journeyed west across the forest to where the Echo Trail runs north and west from near the little township of Ely up to the borders of Canada, driving a narrow wedge of development through the flank of the wilderness. I also stepped straight into the heart of that explosion of light and color known as the American fall.

For a day or two, it was almost more than I could bear. The yellow glow of the birches and aspens, the golden blaze of the tamaracks, the scarlet and orange livery of the maples made fulgent, incandescent with the glory of the sun, seemed to fuse and flame into a brassy arena of light and heat that might at any moment devour me. In time, my senses adjusted to the assault, but for awhile, it was almost with relief that I

welcomed the coming of the night and the soft, velvet shades of dusk.

I do not think we yet realize the full importance and significance of color in our lives. Some research has been done on the subject and some recommendations made, but although we are subconsciously aware of its value and react with pleasure at its stimulus, we do not always realize that it is perhaps vital to our well-being, even our sanity.

I once knew a couple who, for reasons never made quite clear, painted their living quarters sage green. Within a week, they had grown sullen and morose, and by the end of the second week, they had become so irritable and snappish that their relationship was in danger of collapsing. Fortunately, they realized what was happening to them in time, painted their walls bright yellow, and saved their marriage.

In the wild, the deep green mantle of high summer is at first restful and soothing, but leads eventually to a feeling of faint melancholy and depression. The fires of autumn soon cure that, and there is an air of excitement and adventure, a sense of urgency and bustle, which in my case, unaccustomed as I was to such an overdose of color, I found overstimulating.

I was not the only one taking the tonic of the trees, and at weekends particularly, the woods were thronged with people. It was also the season for shooting grouse, those shy, secretive birds of the forest—the ruffed grouse, termed locally, with a fine disregard for scientific classification, partridge. I was told they made splendid eating, and knowing the grouse's epicurean habit of feeding on only the tenderest shoots, flowers, fruits, and seeds, I did not doubt this.

I came upon grouse squatting still as death among the dried fern and litter of the forest floor. Several times, I had to step back to get the bird in focus with my camera. Their ability to merge with their surroundings was superb, and some weeks later, I was to study one transparency many times, wondering why I had taken the picture, only to discover, in the end, the faint outline of a grouse squatting at the base of a log smack in the center of the frame.

I also found beside the trail small bundles of feathers, a handful of entrails, wings, and legs. Most of the hunters dressed their game almost immediately after it was shot, and the practice seemed to me a good one, at least better than nothing. One dawn, I watched as a mink made several forays out on to the trail, each time carrying off some edible morsel that once had been part of a grouse. I had not before thought of the mink as a forager, an opportunity feeder, nor had I realized that it would cache surplus food, yet this seemed to be the object of the exercise.

In another part of the woods, I watched two gray jays feeding on the entrails of a grouse, and from time to time, wiping their beaks in exasperation, trying to rid themselves of the feathers that clung there. I watched a chipmunk bustle to and fro, bearing each time a great mouthful of feathers to some secret underground place. There they would keep the little rodent warm through the frosts of winter, and in time, return to the elements from which they had sprung. Nothing, not a solitary crumb is wasted in the wild. A squirrel will find the remains of the breakfast pancakes, and after dark, in the sun-warmed shallows of the lake, the crayfish will emerge to feed on the fragments washed from the supper plates.

It was, I found, quite dangerous to share the woods with the grouse hunters. Once I had to duck, and let out a most un-grouselike bellow as the shot spattered like hail through the leaves around me. But at least the grouse hunters were legal. It was a different story at night, as cars parked without lights lay in wait along the trail, revealing the presence of illegal hunters wiating for a deer to show itself. Then the very air seemed charged with menace.

After the Boundary Waters Canoe Area, I found the impact

of man on the forest environment somewhat depressing. Neat cabins were dotted about the woods, each with its tank for white gas or central heating oil, its mail box, and carport. It was an environment neither urban, rural, nor wild, but it was as if some alien presence was trying to establish its identity, its right to be there, yet remain apart.

The whole area around Ely bore the scars of man's activity, the taconite mines and their tailings, the highways, the cut-over areas of forest—each in its own way an offense to the eye and wounding to the mind, a monument to man's disregard for the sanctity of the land. By contrast, there was virtually no litter, and coming as I do from one of the untidiest countries in the Western World, I found this pleasing. Occasionally, a roadside litter bin had been upturned by a bear and its contents spilled abroad, but man-made litter was virtually nonexistent.

I found no wolves or any sign of them along the pathways and portages that led off the Echo Trail, and headed south to the banks of the Kawashiwi River to seek the help and guidance of perhaps the world's greatest living authority on the wolf, Dr. L. David Mech. I found a veritable dynamo of a man working with a team of scientists on several projects, including an attempt to arrive at an accurate assessment of wolf populations in the Superior National Forest. To this end, he was attempting to catch individual wolves, equip them with radio collars, and then release them, so that he could follow their future movements by radio. For several days, I accompanied him on his rounds as best I was able, and I was thankful that my weeks in the forest had made me physically fit.

Dr. Mech commiserated with me over my lack of success in coming face to face with a wolf. None knew better than he the unlikelihood of my achieving my goal. He, too, was feeling frustrated, for he had just failed to get the state of Minnesota to agree to award the wolf the status of a game animal.

This may seem a dubious honor to the uninitiated, yet it would have been a considerable leap forward in wolf protection.

At the moment, the wolf in northern Minnesota is regarded as vermin, and it may be hunted, shot, and trapped throughout the year. Only in the Superior National Forest does it enjoy any sort of protection. By making it a game animal, the wolf would be permitted the sanctuary of a closed season. Any hunter who desired to shoot a wolf would be required to purchase a license, and there would be an end to trapping and snaring, insofar as the law could be enforced.

Dr. Mech's total dedication to his work is matched by a complete lack of misplaced sentiment toward animal species of any kind. It was therefore doubly ironic that he should be defeated in his aims largely by the activities of conservationists, animal lovers as vociferous as they were uninformed, who demanded nothing less than complete protection for the wolf. As an ambition, it was laudable enough in its way, but in the face of the great weight of opposition from deerhunters and stock raisers, it was quite impracticable. Both Dr. Mech and I agreed that there were times when it was very difficult to know whose side we were on.

The area in which David Mech was working was a ragged remnant of wilderness, heavily cut over by foresters, intersected by highways, and, in comparison with some areas, quite densely populated, dotted around with numerous cabins, holiday homes, and permanent residences. Working with him, it seemed to me quite incongruous that this world of men should carry another, wilder population, living alongside, yet remaining unseen, unsuspected save for an occasional fleeting gray glimpse.

Yet this area was ideal. The wolves were there, as evidenced by their droppings and the prints of their paws in the mud along the trails. Furthermore, the whole area was interlaced by a veritable maze of old forestry roads, more or less negotiable according to how highly you valued the suspension of your vehicle.

I bounced around for hours in the back of a battered old Chevrolet redolent with the aroma of ripe bait, thrashed through undergrowth that stood shoulder high, and scrambled laboriously over mounds of debris and trash left behind by the loggers. The days were getting shorter. The cries of the Canada geese as they sailed in massive chevron overhead heralded the approach of winter.

I asked David Mech about wolf populations, but like any scientist, he was reluctant to quote figures he was still in the process of trying to verify. He was convinced, however, that the astronomical figures claimed by the antiwolf brigade would prove to be exaggerated. His main concern, at that time, was that many of the wolves he had caught, which had been born in the spring, were not up to the required weight for their age. Food was obviously scarce, and an undernourished cub was unlikely to survive the rigors of its first winter.

My time was nearly up, but there was one more outing in store for me. A graduate student at the research center was working on wolf howls. He was going out that night to howl to the wolves, in the hope that they would howl back. If I liked, I could accompany him. Promptly, I agreed, although secretly filled with stunned disbelief that anyone could be crazy enough to contemplate such a venture, let alone embark on it.

I had an hour or two to spare. I enjoyed a last meal in the forestry campsite nearby, lit a nostalgic last fire, and watched as a yellow-bellied sapsucker made his supper. The sapsucker is an ingenious woodpecker who drills a series of holes—like a cribbage board—in the bark of birch trees. These he visits in turn, to drink the sap, and harvest any insects that might have sheltered there. I watched until the sun set and the sapsucker was a small, dark silhouette against the mirrorlike calm of the lake, and then I doused my fire and returned to the research station.

Once more, I climbed into the back of the Chevvy, and we set off into the forest. The bone-bruising, nerve-wracking, soul-searing, jolting journey went on and on, round and round, up and down, seemingly without object and without end. The unmade roads of the forest carried a maximum speed limit of forty-five miles an hour, and our driver adhered strictly to this limit. Around bends and across potholes, over rocks and boulders, we roared through the night, the twin beams of the headlights cutting a narrow wedge of light into the darkness of the forest. Once, suddenly, we stopped on the summit of a remote and desolate hill, where, a few yards off the track, a spindly radio mast rose in the sky. Gratefully, I climbed out of the van and was just easing my joints back into their accustomed positions when my companions returned, and we were off again.

Throughout the entire evening, the driver's companion wore earphones, plugged into a radio receiver. The object of the exercise, it appeared, was to drive around the forest, covering as wide an area as possible, and all the time listen for a signal that would reveal the close proximity of wolves. Clearly, there was no sense in howling to wolves which might not be there.

Suddenly, with horror, I recognized where we were. We were driving down a hill and at the bottom flowed a creek. Beavers had built a dam across the creek, downstream of the road, and consequently, the road lay under water. The previous day, in broad daylight, we had decided it might be unwise to drive through. Now, it seemed, we were going through it in the dark.

We sailed through in a fine surge of spray, climbed up the slope, and, at once, started to drop downhill again. The driver applied the brakes. Nothing happened. We hit the bottom of the gulley with a bone-jarring crash, the Chevvy lurched, lay down to die, then, changing her mind, crabbed sideways, shook herself, and crawled back on to the road. After that, strangely, I cheered up.

At last, we got the signal we were looking for. The driver parked the van and we moved off into the forest, carrying the recording gear. The night was fine and cold, with no moon or wind, and the stars shone faintly in the sky. We were high on a hill. All around, the forest stretched silent and remote. We came to a flat rock, an island of stone in a sea of undergrowth, and I waited, tense and expectant.

When all was ready, my companions raised their heads and howled. The sound was loud, long-drawn, and, to my ears, most unwolflike. I was conscious of a faint feeling of embarrassment. I waited, but nothing happened, and after an interval, the scientists tried again.

For a moment, nothing stirred. The only sound was the muffled hum of the recording apparatus and the soft whisper of our breathing. Then it happened. Out of the night, out of the black pit of the trees there came the song.

It started softly, a low, wailing threnody that swelled and rose to a throbbing crescendo, a hymn of exultation and joy, then fell away to blend in harmony as voice after voice took up the refrain. Then it was over, and in the silence that followed, I could only stand in awe, for it was as if God and the living forest had spoken.

I knew then that I would return, that one day I would stand in the wilderness and call, and the wolves would answer. Then the words of the ancients would become flesh, for, "They have all one breath."

17

Brief Contact

The long winter passed, in Britain, the mildest and the wettest I could remember. Far away, in Minnesota, the snow was falling. There came a morning in March when I stood on the frozen surface of a lake in the Superior National Forest and looked around me at the snow-clad wilderness. The sun burned my face, but the cold fangs of the wind from the north bit deep into my bones.

I had expected a world of white, and snow there was in plenty, piled in deep drifts beneath the trees, rippling like white sand across the icebound lake, carved and sculpted by the wind into mounds and waves and drifts along the banks of the creeks. Yet there was color, too, vibrant in its beauty, each soft nuance of shade displayed to its best advantage, as though some cosmic jeweler had spread his creative genius over a mantle of white velvet.

The sky was deep blue, paling to silver on the horizon, and the twigs of the birches were purple on the hills. The skeletons of the asters were bone yellow, and each dead seed head held a transient blossom of snow. The fiery red of the dogwood flamed against the mossy green of the pines, and the bark of the birch trees reflected every shade from palest cream to deep, rosy pink. Even the old gray rocks seemed to wear their livery with pride.

I had expected a silent world, but instead, I found a world of soft sounds—the gentle crunch of snowshoes breaking through the crust, the thin high scraping cry of the jays, the lonely call of the crow, and the deep, bell-like note of the raven. Each seemed suspended in time and space, isolated and distinct, to be savored in its purity.

At night, the stars burned down from an indigo sky until the moon rose full and white and dimmed their glory. Then the moon spread a silver pathway over the lake, and the pines stood shrouded in mystery. Each night, I had come down to the lake and stood in the shadows of the trees, waiting and listening, and each night, I had raised my cupped hands to my cheeks and sent the call of the wolf ringing out over the frozen landscape.

To no avail. Once an owl had answered, and the low, wavering call, drifting over the lake, seemed to mock my efforts. Most nights there was just silence, an empty interlude of time in which I strained my ears listening for the faintest echo of my call.

Yet I knew there were wolves in the area. Most days it snowed, at least for an hour or two, and each fresh fall wiped the slate of the wilderness clean. I could be certain that any tracks I saw were fresh, at most no more than a few hours old. I found tracks of fisher, otter, fox, and mink, snowshoe hare, squirrel, and grouse. From time to time, I came upon the tracks and resting places of moose, and I was able to get a fair idea of the moose population in the area. I also found tracks of wolf.

There was clear evidence of a pair, almost certainly a mating couple, plus the prints of a lone wolf, who seemed loosely attached to the pair. I tried to follow them, but snowshoe trailing is slow and arduous work for a novice such as myself, especially through deep snow and dense timber. The wolves, although also handicapped by deep, soft snow, could still move faster than I, even though they had to plunge breast-high through the drifts.

On this March morning, I journeyed down the length of the lake, moving slowly over the ice in the direction of the wooded hills that seemed to dance and beckon but never grow any nearer. The crust was just too soft to bear my weight without snowshoes, and once, when I had tried, I had broken through to a layer of icy slush. I decided not to take any more chances; and so, it was early afternoon before I reached the southernmost shore.

Here, though, I found the evidence I had been seeking ever since I had arrived in the forest, for the whole surface of the lake was crisscrossed with wolf tracks, some large, some small. Within the last few hours, probably during the hours of darkness that had just passed, a wolf pack had scouted the area, checking out every small island and outcrop of rock. Perhaps, even now, they were still close at hand.

Ahead of me, beyond the shore, lay a narrow strip of land, a ridge of high ground with a portage connecting two lakes. Somewhere in these wooded hills, the wolves were lying up, and although it was broad daylight with the sun blazing down from a cloudless sky, I decided to try a wolf call. As usual, feeling slightly foolish, I raised my head and gave cry. Once, twice, three times I called, and then, to my mingled astonishment and delight, the answer came, ringing out from the trees, echoing across the snow, the full-blooded song of a wolf pack.

As the last notes died away and silence fell again across the forest, I was aware of a deep feeling of triumph. This was an achievement far greater than I could have hoped for, a success infinitely superior to gaining a sight of the wolves. Had I spotted a wolf pack before it was aware of my presence, I might have got a fleeting glimpse, even a long view of the animals. But it would have been a one-way affair, an experience unasked for, and unwanted by the wolves.

This was a relationship shared, a contact, a moment of communication, and although perhaps I had deceived the wolves, it had in no way lessened their enjoyment of the occasion, for I knew that wolves loved to sing. Yet I was left with regrets and a hundred questions that might remain forever unanswered. Did I truly deceive the wolves? Were they deluded into believing that another wolf was near, or were they just stimulated by the sound, as I was stimulated by their reply? Scientists even now are working on an analysis of wolf chorusing. Perhaps, one day, I shall know what I said and learn the meaning of the answer.

In the silence that followed, I was uncertain as to what to do next. In the end, I decided that I still wished to get a sight of a wolf. So I made my big mistake.

What I should have done was to stay where I was, hidden myself as well as possible, and then continued calling, softly, in the hope that the wolves would have come to me. Instead, I set off in the direction of the woods, for I knew that the wolves were not more than a hundred yards away.

I must have frightened them off almost at once. I found their tracks in the snow, and the beds where they had lain under the pines, and footprints leading away up into the hills. I looked in vain through the trees, and, after awhile, called again. This time, there was no reply, and at last, wearily, I set off back along the lake, anxious to reach the cabin before dark.

Yet I was not altogether downcast, because I knew that for a brief moment in time the wolves and I had shared a common experience. The idea that we had invoked in each other the same sort of emotion, the same reaction, the same feeling of excitement, might perhaps be dismissed as anthropomorphic, and yet, I am not so sure that the notion can be disposed of so easily.

The wolf and I were alike in more ways than it is possible to enumerate. The same air gave us breath, the same food nourished our blood, the same water quenched our thirst. The same poisons would take our lives, the same anesthetics render us unconscious. The same endocrine glands governed the same behavior patterns, and the same nerve pathways controlled the movements of our facial muscles. Even the foramina in the base of the skull of the wolf matched mine in function and number.

I venture to suggest that if the corpse of a man and that of a wolf were skinned and hung upside down, any observer, although quick to notice differences, would first be struck by similarities. If we were to go further and eviscerate the corpses, then jumble all the organs together in some sort of anatomical jigsaw puzzle, it would take a careful and painstaking operator to reassemble the bodies with their correct parts.

The evidence suggests that we are all no more than different physical manifestations of the same thing. Proof of this lies in the fact that if I put a gosling, a calf, a foal, and a lamb in the same field of grass, I will, in time, get goose down with which to stuff my pillow, leather to make my boots, horsehair with which to make a mattress, and wool from which to weave a blanket, all from the same grass. Furthermore, I know that if I were to die in bed with my boots on, left alone, the whole mass of decomposition would, in time, return to grass.

All this is common, elementary knowledge, shared by every schoolchild, yet still, it seems, we are reluctant to face the truth, preferring, like the Pharisees of old, to rejoice in our differences. Perhaps part of our problem lies in the fact that, today, Homo Sapiens has no mammalian neighbor nearer than the four species of anthropoid apes. Alone on our pinnacle of pride, we feel no true bond with our cousins. So it is that we can have one set of ethics in our relaionships with fellow-man, and another in our relationships with brother wolf.

Yet I wonder what the reaction would be if some remote ancestor, *Australopithecus Africanus,* for example, was discovered to be still extant. Suppose some hunter in an isolated area shot and killed a specimen? Would his crime be hunting without the appropriate license, or would it be murder?

The sun was setting as I reached the end of the lake, staining the snow rose-red and sending dying shafts of light to pierce the gloom of the pines. I was cold, tired, and hungry, but a broad tract of forest still lay between me and the warmth and light of the cabin. I pushed on through the gathering dusk. I noted where a moose had crossed the trail and paused to graze on the shoots of a dogwood tree. It seemed a cold, unpalatable meal with which to end the day.

Then I flushed a grouse from a hollow beneath a cedar tree. It scampered across the snow and exploded in a whirr of wings to lose itself among the pines. At that moment, in contrast to cold dogwood shoots, the thought of hot, raw grouse seemed palatable indeed. Perhaps we are nearer to the wolf, in mentality and outlook, as well as physical form, than we think.

Early man may well have driven away a wolf pack from a kill by pelting it with stones. The wolves could never hope to retaliate by throwing stones back. Their paws are the wrong shape. Yet this in itself does not mean that man and wolf are unalike. Rather it shows that they share a common interest. Like the wolf, man is still prey to his instincts, and while he may not be excessively proud of his legacy from the Pleistocene of such behavior patterns as the desire to gang up, to harry the weaker, more defenseless individual, and to chase anything that runs away, he cannot deny their existence.

Nor, I feel, need he be too ashamed of them, for it was these instincts that were his salvation, that assured his survival down through the years, through harsher, tougher environments than he knows today. One day, perhaps, they may come to his aid once more. Meantime, he need not worry. They will not go away.

18

The Enigma of the Deer

From Duluth to Grand Marais, the wooded borders of Highway 61 were alive with deer. They moved through the trees in wandering bands, stalling under the cedar trees, whose frayed branches, cropped short to a uniform height above the trampled snow, bore mute testimony to their presence.

The white-tailed deer had prospered in the Superior National Forest ever since the great logging era at the beginning of the century. The huge cut-over areas provided an ideal habitat with plenty of cover and ample supplies of browse. So each succeeding year saw an increase in the numbers of deer.

Every winter, they came drifting down out of the forest with the first snows, seeking the warmer climate of the lakeside and the browse which was scarce or absent further inland. The wolf packs, of course, followed them, and many a householder had a stirring tale of wolves hunting deer along the shoreline of the lake, pursuing their prey right up to the very doors of the houses. In recent years, the number of deer arriving for the winter had begun to decline, and many people were convinced that the wolves were to blame.

The decline of the deer appeared to coincide with heavy snowfalls during the winters of 1967, 1968, and 1969. Over the years, it has been the practice of certain individuals to feed the deer in winter, by laying out supplies of hay and alfalfa in their backyards. One Lutzen resident claims that the deer he feeds have dropped from ninety in 1967 to about fifty in recent years. Another man, on the Gunflint Trail, stated that out of eighteen deer feeding at the start of winter, only eight were left by the spring. A lumberjack working along the Manitou River had about thirty deer feeding on the slashings and brush from the logging operations. By spring, only twelve remained.

Certainly, the figures seemed to suggest that wolves were responsible for the decline in deer. They might equally well suggest that wolves found hand-fed deer easy game and sought them out in preference to others, but there could be no proof of this. A more serious consequence of hand-feeding deer was that it encouraged them to hang around the highway. Some two hundred deer a year were killed by automobiles as a result.

Equally concerned about the decline of the deer, although for different reasons, were the deerhunters. A book written during the heyday of big game hunting has this to say about the white-tailed deer:

> As a sporting animal the white-tailed deer is not popular. Mr. Clive Phillips-Wolley describes him as ". . . an exasperating little beast," possessing every quality that a deer ought not to, from the sportsman's point of view. "His haunts are river bottoms, in choking, blinding bush, and his habits are beastly. No one could ever expect to stalk a white-tail; if you want to get one, you must crawl."

Times and opinions change, and today, the white-tailed deer provides sport for a great many hunting either with a rifle or a bow and arrow. The hunters, like those who fed the deer, were convinced that the wolf was to blame for the decline of the white-tail.

It all sounded plausible enough, yet certain facts puzzled me. The thermometer might prove that throughout the winter the climate of the Lake Superior shoreline was on average warmer than that of the interior forest, yet the drafty, windy coast seemed to me a more inhospitable habitat than the windless calm of the woods. Twenty miles to the north, I had seen dense cedar swamps, ideal browse for the deer, where branches swept the snow, undamaged save for the nibblings of snowshoe hares. There not a solitary deer track was to be seen.

I suspected that the deer did not stray far from the highway at any time of year. Indeed, a deer would only have to move a mile into the woods to disappear as effectively as if he had crossed into Canada. I also suspected that the deer haunted the highway, not because it was warmer, but for two other reasons. Firstly, because the going was easier than it would be through deep snow drifts; and secondly, because over the years, they had become accustomed to being fed.

Doubtless, any wolf pack in the area would take its share of deer. It would also defend the territory against other wolf packs, and so to eliminate a wolf pack from a certain area would serve merely to advertise to other wolves that here was a desirable neighborhood to let.

Each timber wolf might be expected to eat the equivalent of twenty-four adult deer in a year. This sounds a lot, but, in 1955, the biologist Milt Stenlund calculated that there were about a hundred and fifty deer per wolf in Minnesota, and it was estimated that wolves were cropping only about sixteen per cent of the herd, far less than the annual birth rate.

Yet now the deer herds were declining, of that there could be no doubt, but to suggest that the wolves were entirely to blame would be to ignore the evidence of ten thousand years—that the predator has always coexisted with its prey. This must surely count for more than a mere lifetime of experience. Certainly the presence of the wolves among the deer would not make their numbers any greater, but there had to be other factors contributing toward the decline, factors which the removal of the wolves might well exacerbate.

There are plenty of men alive who can recall the great numbers of deer that followed in the wake of the logging era, but there are few whose memories go beyond that, to the time before the deer came. Maybe the deer are a once only phenomenon, springing up like fireweed around the ruins of the loggers' camps and the burned-out, cut-over areas of forest. Maybe their era is passing, and the deer are giving way, not to the wolves, but to the living forest.

There are those who maintain that there is still plenty of browse for the deer and who point out that, over the past twenty years, the forest service has planted more than fifty-two million trees. Yet the deer spread through the forest, not because men planted trees, but because they cut them down. Now perhaps, the deer can serve the environment no more, and so are abdicating in favor of other herbivores, more suited to serve the domain and so more likely to survive. In a sense, the deer are as much parasitic to the forest as the tapeworm to the deer. Each species hastens its own end.

No matter how precious the deer might be as hunting trophies, scenic attractions, or food for the wolves, it may be that in concerning ourselves too greatly about his future in the Superior National Forest, we have got our priorities wrong. Like many Englishmen, I own a garden, in places semiwild, a feature due in part to sheer neglect, in part to a desire to share my plot with the rest of the living world. One year, I planted a fire thorn, an evergreen shrub with masses of brilliant red berries. The first winter, my fire thorn bore seventeen berries, and after the first snowfall, a redwing came and ate the lot. I had to wait another year to discover just how many berries a redwing can eat.

I learned that they regularly took twenty-four at a sitting, and each year now, my fire thorn is stripped within a month of ripening. My neighbors ask me why I don't put a net over the tree or scare the birds away, and my answer is simple. Anyone can grow a fire thorn, but not everyone can enjoy the sight of redwings, bright against the snow. A garden is not just a place to grow flowers, but a harbor of sanctuary and peace, for all things.

I have too, a pond, where fat carp swim among the water lilies, and frogs and newts live. I also have the biggest grass snake I have ever seen. At least, she comes and goes, and eats the frogs, and occasionally, one of the carp. Yet again, I console myself with the thought that anyone can keep carp. Not everyone is privileged to share his garden with a grass snake.

Throughout the whole of the Eastern United States, as far south as Louisiana, the white-tailed deer is on the increase. Many states can brag of deer; few can boast of moose. Only Michigan and Minnesota can claim the eastern timber wolf. For how long depends upon the people of those states. Meanwhile, it is vital that we at least try to ascertain the facts about deer and wolf populations, even bearing in mind that the truth, when it finally does emerge, may be unpalatable, for scientific fact is cold and no respecter of theory, however long cherished.

In a way, such research is to be regretted. As a naturalist, it has been my lifelong principle to keep my hands to myself. I consider it my privilege to look, but not to tamper. I am aware that even as a spectator, my presence might well disturb that which I am intent on watching. It is impossible to move, no matter how softly, through the environment without sending out small ripples of cause and effect.

So it is that I can never contemplate research into animal populations, with all the ringing and tagging and sampling that scientific exploration calls for, without a faint sense of outrage, without the thought that man, for all he may give himself airs, is little more than a meddling, poking, prying ape, forever sticking his fingers where they are not wanted. Yet at the same time, I must admit that this is the only way to learn for certain whether a wolf or deer population is increasing or declining. For the moment, the end must justify the means.

There is another, more cogent reason why we must study the relationship of wolf/deer dynamics. The deer came to the forest as the result of a change, and in nature, as in all life, the result of one change is the cause of another. In the last few hundred years, the face of the Northlands has changed so often that it is almost impossible to stand in any one place and say, "This is how things should be."

This state of affairs is not confined to the Northlands; the problem is world-wide. Each autumn in Britain, the rains lash the land, and the rivers race to the sea, red with suspended silt, the fertile topsoil of our fields. It has been so all my life, and in my father's life, and in his father's before that. No one stops to wonder whether it should be so, whether it is natural or normal that it should happen. Indeed, our agriculturists and water engineers hasten the process by land drainage and by straightening the rivers in the cause of flood prevention. No one stops to wonder whether we are not impoverishing the land, yet we only have to look at other, older civilizations to see the poverty and ruination that erosion brings. We do not believe it can happen to us, for we have no norm, no standard, no natural datum line with which to compare. So each winter, I stand on the hill and watch the blood of the land spill out in a waving red banner to the sea.

Once, to illustrate an article, I went out to try and take a photograph of my environment untouched or unharmed by man. I searched for a long time, through fields and along rivers, over moorland and mountain and forest. I got my picture, in the end, in a tiny rock pool left by the ebbing tide.

There are few places left untouched by man, and such as there are grow yearly more precious. All around us, the land is sick. We have exhausted it, and debilitated it, and exposed it to disease, but as yet, only a few see the symptoms, and even they do not know how critical they are. Only in the few wild areas remaining, in environments which are healthy, can we learn what is whole and what is unwell.

Other areas, which in the past have been violated and misused, still retain the capacity for recovery. My impression of the Superior National Forest was that this was one of those areas. It might take a thousand years, but this, although long in the lifetime of man, is but a short spell in the history of the human race. It would, at least, be a living monument to our ideals. It would, too, be a small enough sacrifice. Though vast, the forest is but a minute fraction of the great continent of North America.

I left the deer by the roadside, placidly ruminating over their mounds of hay, and went back into the forest. A pair of moose, a cow and her calf, had crossed an inlet of the lake in my absence. Their massive hoofprints, sunk deep into the snow, vanished into the forest. There was no evidence that a wolf pack had harried them, and so I presumed they were just changing their feeding grounds.

It is probably true to say that no herbivore on this planet is by choice an habitual grazer. Each is at heart a browser, grazing when opportunity presents itself or when force of circumstance compels it. There is an important distinction between the two feeding patterns, for the grazer, cropping the short grass of meadow and mountain, may feed only as far as it may wander, and the coming of winter means that it must scratch beneath the snow in search of sustenance or starve.

For the browser, no such problems arise. It may graze when the grass is lush and green, but the coming of the snow does not deprive it of food. As well as finding fodder as far as it can roam, it can also find nourishment as high as it can reach. Just as the shelves of the supermarket hold more goods than the conventional store, so the forest contains a greater quantity and range of goods than the pasture.

The moose is better equipped to dine off the forest than the deer. Its legs are longer, serving to carry it safely through deep snow. Its height is greater and its neck longer, so it can reach fodder that is far above the deer's head. It is also stronger and so can crop shoots and small branches too tough for the deer's jaws. All these factors not only work in favor of the moose, they are also of benefit to the forest, for the forest, as a living entity, strives always to avoid growing to a climax.

As living proof, moose are increasing in numbers throughout the whole of the Superior National Forest. Are moose responsible for the decline of the deer, or rather, are they a contributory factor, together with the slow maturation of the forest? Is a moose territorially minded enough to drive off any deer in the vicinity? It is a trait I can well imagine being in keeping with the behavior of an irascible bull moose. Again is it significant that twelve deer introduced onto Isle Royale, in 1906, at a time when the moose population was increasing, all disappeared?

The answers to these questions may one day be found, but first they have to be asked. Meantime, I must curb my impatience and my natural distaste at the way such inquiries are carried out, reminding myself that the scientists investigating these matters are as dedicated to the truth as I am, and, on the whole, are possessed of infinitely more stamina and patience.

Reflecting on the decline of the white-tailed deer, I remember a conversation I had with a forest ranger. Discussing the cattlemen's antipathy to the wolf, he said, "Nobody in his right mind would try to raise bananas up here. Maybe we shouldn't be trying to raise cattle either."

Nor, perhaps, should we be trying to raise deer.

19

Fate Plays the Joker

More deer die as a result of being knocked down by automobiles on Highway 61 than are killed by wolves on the mainland of Michigan. Each winter, more than two hundred casualties are reported—some killed outright, some so severely wounded as to warrant immediate destruction. The deer remain the propery of the state, and where possible, the meat is handed over to families who are poor enough to need the aid of the welfare department.

The conservation officer turned one such carcass over to me, a doe so horribly mangled as to be unfit for human consumption. The same night we dragged it out across the frozen lake, and staked it out on a small rocky islet, exposed and treeless, but close enough to cover to enable me to watch over it.

I had lost contact with the wolf pack. They had moved away southwest, too far into the trackless wilderness of forest for me to follow. Yet I lived in hopes that they might return, and meanwhile, there was still the pair and the lone wolf lingering in the neighborhood. I hoped that the dead deer would lure the wolves to feed, for once again, my time was running out, and I had but a few days left in which to fulfill my ambitions. In a way, I was relieved that the large pack was not present, for they would demolish the whole carcass very rapidly, no doubt at a time when I was not present.

Next morning, I was up before dawn. During the night, the temperature had fallen lower than at any time during my stay, and as I moved across the lake in the subzero temperature, the moisture in my nostrils froze with every indrawn breath.

As quietly as possible I approached the kill, taking advantage of the dead ground to conceal me from the eyes of anything that might be feeding. What faint breeze there was blew in my face. Just below the summit of the rise, I hollowed out a couch in the deep snow and then peered cautiously out.

The deer lay untouched, just as we had left it the night before. I waited until the sun was high above the pines and my fingers were numb with the threat of frostbite, but nothing came near. No tracks led to or from the carcass. Reluctantly, I returned to the cabin, to a roaring fire, and a large breakfast.

Late in the afternoon, I tried again. I had reckoned without the ravens. During the day, they had found the kill and had flocked to the feast. Those whose crops would hold no more hung like tattered black flags to the treetops, and my approach was greeted by a derisive chorus of hoots and honks. Since my presence was well and truly betrayed, I did not bother to linger, but stayed only to check that the carcass had not been visited. All round, the snow was clear of prints.

There was a second vantage point, not nearly so close, but one which could be approached under cover of the trees. For two days, I waited and watched; and meantime, the weather worsened. In spite of the intense cold, more snow fell, and a strong wind blew from the northwest across the lake, straight into my face.

It became impossible to watch for more than a few minutes

at a time without turning away to wipe the tears from my eyes—tears that blinded me and threatened to freeze on my cheeks. At least the ravens, which continued to feed, oblivious of my presence, were enjoying themselves; deer hair lay spread in a wide area around the carcass, and hourly, the deer seemed to sink deeper into the snow.

By the third morning, I was discouraged enough to forgo the dawn start. Nothing had visited the carcass save ravens and crows; furthermore, I had seen no sign of wolves anywhere in the vicinity. As I set off across the lake just before noon, a blizzard began to blow, until, at last, the visibility grew so poor that I doubted whether I would even be able to see the kill. Once in the shelter of the trees, however, conditions did not seem too bad, and I pushed on, following the now well-beaten trail.

Fate, I sometimes feel, is a cardsharp. Furthermore, when she deals from the bottom of the pack, it is not with the intention of winning, but simply for the pleasure of witnessing the consternation of the players when they see their cards. On this particular morning, she had an interesting hand in store for me.

I reached the lake shore and crouched behind the fallen cedar that screened me from view. The wind blew stronger than ever, and the snow whirled past, stinging my eyelids and obscuring the lens of my camera. I peered out to the barely visible carcass.

The ravens were in attendance as usual, but there was something else as well—a large, black bulk that crouched over the kill, its size not only dwarfing that of the ravens but also the remains of the deer. For a moment, my heart leaped, for I was sure that my ambition had been realized. Then I saw that it was not a wolf but an eagle, an American bald eagle, rarer by far, in the Superior National Forest, than the wolf.

Like all birds of prey, the bald eagle has been declining in

numbers over recent years. Although still fairly well established in Alaska, over the rest of the United States there are
only several hundred breeding pairs. What this particular specimen was doing so far north so early in the year, I could not
imagine. By rights, it should be hunting along the open shores
of the Missouri rather than trying to survive in this frozen
forest. The lake would not be free of ice for at least another six
weeks, and until then, the chief food of the eagle, fish, would
not be available.

I watched the mighty bird feed for a long time, taking what
pictures I could through the screen of driving snow. Then as
the eagle took flight and soared into the sky, I stepped out onto
the lake and took one last shot. These pictures are without
doubt the worst, and most precious, in my collection.

So ended my last chance to see a wolf, for the next day,
my journey led toward Chicago and a jet plane back to Britain.
In a sense, I had failed in my mission, for I never did get to
see a wild wolf. Yet I had been close to them, closer than
many men, not just in the physical sense of being nearby, but
in bridging a void wider than that ever faced by the explorers
of old.

Furthermore, and in this I was well content, I had been in-
strumental in returning to the living forest a tiny fragment of
the wealth that was its due. In time, the elements that were
once a living deer would be transmuted back into twig and leaf
and berry and fern. I had helped a bald eagle in its struggle for
survival, and perhaps, even as I write, somewhere in the North
woods there is an eagle chick whose fate, by some strange
alchemy, is linked to mine.

I had also solved a riddle, and the answer when it was
revealed, was, like the solution to every conundrum, so obvious that I could only feel astonishment that I had not perceived
it before. For I now knew that my destiny, and that of other
men, together with life in all its variety of manifestation, could

only be assured in service to the rest of the living world. The reason why was not to be revealed, but I knew I was bound by the inescapable law.

For I had shared the wilderness experience, and it is not possible to go into the wilderness and emerge unchanged. I know this now, and I know that it will call me back. It is a small voice, and far away, but it is insistent and impelling, and I cannot escape the sound, so there will come a time when I can ignore it no longer and must return. Then I will feel again the aching and the weariness as my body slowly attunes itself to the demands of the wild until it is fit and hard and obedient to my will. I will feel the burn of sun and wind, the cool caress of the rain, and the ground springing beneath my feet. I will smell the odor of pine and water, and wood smoke and earth, and hear the silence, punctuated by the voices of the wild. I will live.

I am one with my environment, mind and body, spirit and matter. Out of the earth I came, and to the earth I shall return. I am an ear of wheat and the leaf of the aspen. My bones are the bones of long dead warriors, and my blood is the ore fused in the rocks by the first fires of creation. The flesh of the dinosaur and the mammoth, of Neanderthal man and the peoples of ancient Rome, the buffalo and the blue whale, and the dead of a hundred wars live again in me and my kind, transmuted a thousand times on their journey through time and space.

This is the lesson of the wilderness, and it is not enough just to state it. The lesson has to be learned, through hardship and endurance and isolation, until, with the passage of time and distance, you not only lose the sense of where you are but who and what you are. Then, with a new-found humility and innocence, you can lie on the warm, soft earth, and with your face to the sky, merge and blend with the universe.

To be what you are. To discover anew the tranquility of having no identity, to be free from the pressures and demands of a social system that calls upon an individual endlessly to act a part. This is the wilderness experience; a cleansing and a rebirth, a mental and physical adjustment far deeper and more profound than the mere pleasure of physical recreation, and the enjoyment of new and beautiful surroundings.

There are those who believe that man will destroy himself, and in so doing, bring about the destruction of the rest of the living world. I cannot share such a gloomy view. No doubt civilizations will fall and life patterns change, but out of the holocaust, a new breed of man will emerge. There may well come a time when the ancient prophecy will be fulfilled, and the meek shall inherit the earth.

From the smoldering ruins of the cities and the devastation and defoliation of the farmlands, the survivors will emerge to turn again to the wilderness, to that which is clean and pure and healthy, and learn to live again.

Meantime, mankind will continue to seek out the wild places, to become again true servants of the environment, to abide by its laws. Some, through error or misjudgment, will die there. This could be no bad way to end a life, and for my part, I would ask for nothing better than to lie on some long-forgotten hillside, until the flowering grasses make seeds of my bones.

Those who return to civilization, who come back to face their responsibilities and dependents, will declare themselves rejuvenated and revitalized, fired with fresh inspiration. They may speak more truly than they know, for it may be that this life force which we are conceited enough to believe emanates from within ourselves is absorbed and inspired rather than metabolized, is a force with which we are imbued, rather than one which we generate. For we are what the philosophers of old said we were, earth and air, fire and water, and the more we try to insulate ourselves with concrete and plastic, and artificial light and air conditioning, the less we live.

One last time, I stood on the frozen surface of the lake. The snow had stopped falling and the stars glittered in the sky, while all around the frost held the forest in its icy grip. Once more, I raised my voice in farewell to the moose, to the ravens and the eagle, to the wolf I never saw. The pilgrimage was over.

Postscript

Since I wrote these words the timber wolf in Minnesota is now protected by state statutes complying with the Federal Endangered Species Act of 1973, so that wolves cannot now be taken, possessed or sold except under a permit from the state commissioner of natural resources.

Fires have raged through the Superior National Forest following an exceptionally dry and windy spring, and brown bears have increased so much that they have been a torment to campers and a worry to conservation officers. . . . The pattern of forest life continues to grow on the loom of time.